INTERLIBRARY LOAN PRACTICES HANDBOOK

# INTERLIBRARY LOAN PRACTICES HANDBOOK

THIRD EDITION

Edited by Cherié L. Weible and Karen L. Janke

AMERICAN LIBRARY ASSOCIATION • CHICAGO 2011

**Cherié L. Weible** is head of Interlibrary Loan and Document Delivery at the University of Illinois at Urbana-Champaign and has been in the department for eleven years. Cherié is an associate professor at the university and has published twenty-four articles, presented twenty-five papers and lectures, and consulted for ILL operations workflow on a professional level. She holds an MA in history from Pittsburg State University (Kansas) and an MS in Library and Information Science from the University of Illinois at Urbana-Champaign.

**Karen L. Janke** is the library director at Erikson Institute, a graduate school in child development located in downtown Chicago, where she has worked since July 2009. Previously, Karen was an associate librarian and team leader for Access Services at Indiana University-Purdue University Indianapolis, where she worked for eight years in Interlibrary Loan and Access Services after receiving her MLS from the University of Illinois in 2001. She has coauthored two articles for the *Journal of Interlibrary Loan, Document Delivery and Electronic Reserve* on article delivery turnaround time and management issues as well as a forthcoming article in the *Journal of Popular Culture*.



Printed in the United States of America
15 14 13 12 11 5 4 3 2 1



ISBNs: 978-0-8389-1081-8 (paper); 978-0-8389- 9294-4 (PDF); 978-0-8389- 9295-1 (ePub); 978-0-8389- 9296-8 (Mobipocket); 978-0-8389- 9297-5 (Kindle). For more information on digital formats, visit the ALA Store at alastore.ala.org and select eEditions.

**Library of Congress Cataloging-in-Publication Data**
Boucher, Virginia, 1929–
Interlibrary loan practices handbook / [Virginia Boucher] ; [edited by] Cherié L. Weible and Karen L. Janke. — 3rd ed.
p. cm.
Includes bibliographical references and index.
Previous ed.: 1997.
ISBN 978-0-8389-1081-8 (alk. paper)
1. Interlibrary loans—United States—Handbooks, manuals, etc. I. Weible, Cherié L. II. Janke, Karen L. III. Title.
Z713.5.U6B68 2011
025.6'2—dc23

2011017433

Cover design by Casey Bayer. Interior design in Scala and ScalaSans by Adrianna Sutton.

♾ This paper meets the requirements of ANSI/NISO Z39.48-1992 (Permanence of Paper).

# CONTENTS

# FOREWORD

WHEN I STEPPED into interlibrary loan (ILL) at the University of Colorado at Boulder Libraries in 1967, the service was open only to faculty and graduate students. Reference sources, especially bibliographies, were important as a source of information. Locations for libraries holding materials were discovered at a statewide center (union card catalog), the *National Union Catalog*, or the Library of Congress. Typewritten four-part paper forms were a great way to send and keep track of requests. There was no OCLC or other electronic ILL system. There was a national ILL code but no Colorado code. There also seemed to be nobody at all whom I could ask for enlightenment concerning ILL.

As the years slipped by, I learned enough to help others. I conducted many workshops, gave speeches, organized conferences, and did a two-day seminar at the University of Wisconsin School of Library and Information Studies nine different times. The *Interlibrary Loan Practices Handbook* was published twice—once while I was working and once after retirement. (By the way, the current cat is all black and named Zorro.)

Since my retirement the ILL world has changed dramatically. The individual's need for information (and entertainment) has continued unabated while methods for producing materials seem to proliferate daily. One must keep up with all new developments. This book will give a current perspective and help for the neophyte.

A constant remains, however, and it is the most important thing about ILL: *people*. Those who need the materials and those who supply them are an endless panoply of interest and sometimes excitement. And so, to quote myself: "Cherish your family, value your colleagues, and whether it be in person or electronically, treat kindly those who come to you for help."

*Virginia Boucher*
*Professor of Libraries, Emerita*
*University of Colorado at Boulder*

# PREFACE

I WAS BOTH surprised and honored when I was approached to produce the third edition of the ILL *Handbook*. Unlike Virginia Boucher who single-handedly created two wonderful editions, I felt that I needed to call on a little help from my ILL friends. The first person I contacted was Karen Janke, a trusted colleague, a good writer and editor, and someone I knew I could work with well. Thank you, Karen, for helping to make this edition of the ILL *Handbook* happen!

This edition of the handbook covers the basics of ILL and is aimed at the new practitioner as well as those who have suddenly found themselves responsible for an ILL unit. We didn't want the writing to be overly prescriptive, but we did want enough basic details so that someone who found himself or herself working in an ILL unit would have some idea of how to get through the job!

I also want to thank each of our chapter contributors. We chose a variety of contributors, some who have been in the field for decades and some newer, because fresh ideas and new energy are always valued in ILL. We and the chapter authors have a combined 158 years of experience in ILL!

*Cherié L. Weible*

I BECAME AN ILL practitioner exactly ten years ago, quite by accident: I was a graduate student at the University of Illinois Graduate School for Library and Information Science, I needed a summer job, and the ILL department was hiring. However, I quickly learned to love the chaos: requests were constantly coming in and there was always something to do. The process of interlibrary loan captured my imagination, and perhaps the simplest thing inspired me to think about the work I was doing in my library and what was happening in libraries all over the world. The simple thing was the ILL request number created when you submitted a request on the OCLC ILL system. This was back in the day of OCLC's Prism. Using that program made me feel like I belonged to a keystroke-based, command-driven secret society: 3,2,2,1 or 4,4 anyone? Even if you were a savvy searcher and fast typist, hundreds or thousands of new requests could be created by other libraries in the brief moments between your requests. And you knew this because of that request number, the sequential indication of just how busy we all were. You know you're an addict when you start to daydream what it might take to achieve the ultimate: sequential ILL request numbers.

Another amazing realization was that interlibrary loan was the concept of a lending library writ large: libraries sending their materials simply because another library submitted a request, and trusting that they would be returned unharmed. No user was at a disadvantage if her library didn't have the specific item she needed, because in the vast majority of cases another library was willing to help. At times I felt that it was a small miracle that a request could be filled at all. Given that so many people touched some aspect of a request from beginning to end, it seemed that there was a lot of room for error. But all it takes is one library to say yes. In the ten years since then, I have learned so much from other interlibrary loan colleagues. We are a creative, collaborative group of people, and we succeed in our mission of meeting our patrons' needs because of each other. Even though technological advances have revolutionized the mechanics of the ILL request process in the past ten years, the spirit of trusting and helping remains.

*Karen L. Janke*

CHAPTER ONE

# INTERLIBRARY LOAN
## EVOLUTION TO REVOLUTION

*Margaret W. Ellingson and Susan D. Morris*

MANY LIBRARY STAFF MEMBERS today have the impression that resource sharing in general and interlibrary loan (ILL) in particular are relative newcomers to the library scene. After all, how could libraries systematically locate and obtain requested items without the Internet, computers, and scanners? In fact, resource sharing and interlibrary loan have a long-established place among library services that is traceable to ancient times. Interlibrary loan transactions through the ages have been conducted with an ever-evolving array of "technologies" to carry out the familiar processes of identifying, locating, requesting, and delivering items desired by library users. And from the earliest days, familiar issues such as bad citations, difficult users, technological glitches, overburdened lenders, costs, and copyright have challenged participants in the interlibrary loan process.

On the one hand, tracing the evolution of ILL reveals the truth of the old saying that "the more things change, the more they stay the same." On the other hand, it can help us to understand the developments that have dramatically altered both user expectations regarding interlibrary loan and the ability of libraries to respond in an ever-changing environment.

### IN THE BEGINNING . . .

The roots of interlibrary loan were established thousands of years ago. In Western civilization, writing was invented between 3400 and 3000 BC in today's southern Iraq. The technology was the material at hand—clay tablets with styluses. The works created were not histories, philosophies, or epic legends; however, while seemingly mundane, they were still of vital importance to their users—business transactions, rosters of names, and other official records.

These records sometimes required duplication and delivery elsewhere. People later realized that the processes of recording and copying could also be applied to histories and legends. Eventually, specialized workers called scribes established their place as valued members of society, spending their lives recording, copying, and making the distribution of information possible.

New technologies continued evolving to make information sharing easier. Clay tablets got the job done, but they were both heavy and fragile. Scrolls fashioned from papyrus and leather were a much lighter medium, easier to manipulate and more durable for transport. To record information on this medium, ink was invented.

Scrolls were collected and housed in buildings constructed specifically for their storage. When it burned during the age of Caesar, the legendary library of Alexandria in Egypt was home to tens of thousands of scrolls. Some scrolls had been added through confiscation from passing ships. Others were added when Ptolemy III (246–221 BC) wrote to the known world's sovereigns asking to borrow their scrolls for copying. He deposited a bond—what we might call a loan fee—to cover expenses and ensure the safety of the items in transit, but he often kept both original and copy, thus making himself one of history's earliest known problem patrons![1]

During the next thousand years or so, the monasteries of the European Middle Ages adopted the use of skins worked into vellum as their writing medium. Hand-inscribed and gorgeously embellished with illuminations, these sheets were bound into today's familiar codex—or book—format. Copying, swapping, and lending books were thriving activities. However, an exchange of letters between Lull, Bishop of Mainz, and Guthbert, Abbot of Wearmouth-Jarrow, gives us a glimpse into medieval technological glitches. Lull had requested copies of a list of works concerning Bede the Venerable, one of England's foremost scholars. Guthbert, whose cloister was home to Bede, apologized to Lull saying that, of the many items on the list, Guthbert could only manage to supply a single biography of Bede, because his own hands and those of his other copyists had been paralyzed by the unusually cold winter of 763–764.[2] The medieval copy machine was out of order, and ILL requests could not be filled!

Two technological advances soon provided a quantum leap in information sharing. Paper, brought to Europe from China, was faster and cheaper to produce than vellum. Movable type, popularized by Johannes Gutenberg around 1460, further revolutionized the ability to duplicate and spread information more quickly and efficiently than ever before. While the privileged classes continued to amass great private collections, over the next four centuries more and more commoners could afford books. Libraries proliferated—in universities, in offices of individual scholars, and, finally, in cities and towns for the benefit of the general population. Catalogs became recognized as more than mere inventory lists; Gabriel Naudé, a French librarian, stated in 1627 that catalogs can direct friends to an owning library if their own library lacks the desired book.[3]

In the late nineteenth century, Germany was unified into a single country. It became a leader in the rapidly developing science and technology of the time and was among the first of modern European countries to regard the functions of a library in a professional way. The Germans designed libraries with reading rooms for users and processing areas for staff. They also realized that the methodical nature of German scholarship, coupled with German principles of cataloging and multiple access points, made interlibrary loan as a formalized process both necessary and possible. Nationalization throughout Europe during the eighteenth and nineteenth centuries resulted in most countries designating an official national library, including the British Library in the United Kingdom and the Bibliothèque nationale de France.

## "NATIONAL" LIBRARY DEVELOPMENT

Though the United States has no official national library, the Library of Congress (LC) serves as our country's de facto national library. As early as 1776, the Continental Congress authorized a congressional library, but legislation providing for its creation did not pass until 1800. In the mid- to late 1800s, Congress authorized LC to be a copyright depository and to administer copyright law; as a result, its collection began to grow exponentially. Today, the Library of Congress is arguably the largest library in the world. In the late 1960s LC embraced the MARC (MAchine-Readable Cataloging) format, providing the big push needed to make library automation possible. Two results of the MARC format are online bibliographic records and online ILL systems. Because the original mission of LC was to serve the information needs of the U.S. Congress, LC is a library of last resort for interlibrary loan by libraries both at home and abroad.

What was to become the first true national library in the United States began modestly in 1836 with a $50 request for medical books for the Office of the Surgeon General of the Army. In 1864, at the height of the Civil War, the library issued its first printed catalog of approximately 2,100 volumes. After the Civil War, numerous Army hospitals closed and sent their collections of medical books and journals to the Surgeon General's office. John Shaw Billings was appointed as the librarian to deal with this windfall of medical material. By the time he resigned in 1895, Billings had assembled the world's greatest medical library collection, consisting of 116,847 books and 191,598 pamphlets and encompassing the medical literature of all nations and eras to date. In so doing, Billings laid the foundation for today's National Library of Medicine (NLM), including actively lending books and journals to physicians across the country. Congress passed legislation in 1956 that formed the basis for an expanded interlibrary loan program at NLM. Subsequent legislation in 1965 established, among other programs, eleven Regional Medical Libraries that still provide ILL and other services within their regions.

The Department of Agriculture library opened in 1862 with a collection of one thousand volumes. By 1934, with a collection of over 250,000 volumes, the library began participating in the Bibliofilm Service, the first large-scale attempt by a library to provide microfilm copies of articles to scientific researchers, rather than lending the original documents. In its first year, this program distributed over 300,000 copies. In 1962, on the one hundredth anniversary of the library's establishment, the library was officially designated the National Agricultural Library (NAL), making it the third national library in the United States. Over the years NAL has participated in a variety of resource-sharing programs, including coordination of a national network of state land-grant and U.S. Department of Agriculture (USDA) field libraries. NAL participates in ILL as a library of last resort.

## NINETY-THREE YEARS OF EVOLUTION: ILL IN THE UNITED STATES, 1876–1969

Throughout the first three-quarters of the nineteenth century, an increase in the number of public and academic libraries in the United States and in the development of librarianship as a profession laid the foundation for further advancement in resource sharing.

## 1876–1899

Informal resource sharing undoubtedly occurred among U.S. libraries from colonial times through the early years of the republic. In the nineteenth century, the idea of formalized interlibrary loan steadily gained strength in North America, influenced by what was happening in Europe. By 1876, the year that the American Library Association (ALA) was founded, Samuel Green of the Worcester (Massachusetts) Free Public Library wrote in the very first issue of the *American Library Journal*:

> It would add greatly to the usefulness of our reference libraries if an agreement should be made to lend books to each other for short periods of time . . . . I should think libraries would be willing to make themselves responsible for the value of borrowed books, and be willing to pay an amount of expressage that would make the transportation company liable for the loss in money should the books disappear in transit. . . . I am informed that a plan of this kind is in operation in Europe. . . . Perhaps the matter is worthy the consideration of the Conference of Librarians at Philadelphia?[4]

On the page following Green's letter pleading for consideration of interlibrary loan as a legitimate activity of libraries, "library cooperation" was listed as one of the topics for discussion at the Philadelphia Conference.

Some twenty years later, in the October 1898 edition of *Library Journal*, Green updated his experience with interlibrary loan and made suggestions to improve the process:

> [T]he first instance of a general and systematic plan in this country of loaning books to out-of-town libraries was that . . . acted upon in the great medical and surgical library of the Surgeon-General's Office. . . . I frequently borrow from the library of the Surgeon-General's Office. . . . I have sent for books to a place as far away from Worcester as Detroit. . . . I have had a precious and unique manuscript entrusted to me by the custodian of one of the law libraries of Boston for the use of a special student. . . . I am of the opinion that the system of library inter-loaning should be more widely extended and that small libraries should lend to one another as well as the smaller libraries borrowing from larger ones. . . . [T]hey (the smaller libraries) should be on the lookout for opportunities to help the larger libraries.[5]

With the seeds of formalized resource sharing firmly planted by the last quarter of the nineteenth century, we will next examine the evolution, and later the revolution, of interlibrary loan in the United States, exploring four main areas of development—codes, cooperation and consortia, technology, and copyright—from 1876 to the present.

### *Codes*

Though formal codes were still decades away, Samuel Green laid out several ideas that eventually became the foundations of ILL codes in the United States, noting that certain problems could be avoided by "enforcing rules dictated by common sense."[6] Besides the notions of reciprocity and load leveling, he also discussed the special nature of scholarly interlibrary loan, the responsibilities of the borrower, the lender's right to exclude or restrict certain materials, and the need to cover mailing costs.

*Cooperation and Consortia*
The development of cooperative groups, or consortia, occurred partly to help libraries cope with technological advances, concern with copyright, and costs of materials and services. The proliferation of consortia has proved to be both product and producer of advancements, as we shall see in tracing their development throughout the twentieth century. Two major developments in the latter part of the nineteenth century set the tone for library cooperation as we still know it. In 1876 the American Library Association (ALA) was founded, signaling the beginning of significant national library cooperation in the United States. The need for more localized cooperation was also recognized, and in July 1890, the New York State Library Association was founded. One of its four objectives was "to organize and promote among New York libraries . . . interlibrary loans and other forms of cooperation."[7] Before the decade was over, states as far-flung as New Hampshire, Iowa, and Georgia had also established state associations.

*Technology*
As early as 1839 the processes of photography and microphotography were being developed in France. A prototype of the first fax machine was given a patent in Scotland in 1843. Production of a commercially viable typewriter began in 1873. Carbon paper, first invented around 1806, found a practical use as the typewriter grew in popularity, and by 1877 the value of the typewriter as a cataloging aid was debated at ALA.

Other forms of data transfer included the linotype machine, invented in 1884. Libraries such as the Public Library of New London, Connecticut, experimented with printing and distributing finding lists, thus reducing the practice of "blind" requesting interlibrary loans.

The first "online" interlibrary cooperation occurred in 1897: the Boston Public Library provided a telephone information service utilizing stenographers to contact other libraries by phone and to furnish patrons with typed verbatim copies or abstracts of requested documents.

*Copyright*
In 1787 a provision for copyright appeared in the newly ratified U.S. Constitution, followed by the implementation of the Copyright Act of 1790. During the nineteenth century a series of court rulings shaped revisions to U.S. copyright law. The 1841 case of *Folsom v. Marsh* stands out in that it resulted in a ruling forming the basis of the "fair use" doctrine. During the latter half of the nineteenth century, the need for mutual recognition of copyright between sovereign nations grew more and more apparent. In 1886 the Berne Convention first met for this purpose. The United States, however, did not sign the Berne Convention until over one hundred years later, in 1988.

## 1900–1949

*Codes*
Despite Samuel Green's 1876 recommendation that librarians formalize interlibrary loan procedures in the United States, the ALA Committee on Co-ordination did not submit the first *Code of Practice for Interlibrary Loans* for approval until 1917. This code, with minor modifications, was approved in 1919. The committee chairman characterized the code as embodying "the more essential points in

the actual practices of those libraries in North America which are now the chief lenders to other libraries" and further stated that "compliance with its recommendations will entail no departure from well recognized procedure."[8] Significantly, subsequent interlibrary loan codes have been written in the same vein—attempting mainly to codify current library practice rather than to break new ground.

Many of the provisions of the relatively brief and surprisingly liberal 1917 code are still in practice. This first U.S. code espoused interlibrary lending not only to aid research but also to "augment the supply of the average book to the average reader" and went on to say that "it may be assumed that all libraries are prepared to go as far as they reasonably can . . . in lending to others."[9] In addition, the code incorporated the concept of reproduction in lieu of a loan and encouraged the use of legible, complete, and accurate citations, reasonable loan periods, and notice of receipt and return of materials. The code further stated that the borrowing library was responsible for requested material, even in transit, and that lenders could suspend service to libraries that disregard provisions of the code. Costs were also addressed by the first code, which stipulated that the entire cost of shipping and insurance, if applicable, was the responsibility of the borrowing library.

Subsequent changes in academic and library environments, including war-related research and publication, spurred significant increases in interlibrary loan activity and prompted revisions to the original 1917 *Code of Practice*. A new interlibrary loan code, with significant input from apparently overburdened research libraries, was approved in 1940. This code was significantly longer and more restrictive than the 1917 code in an attempt to address increasing costs and other "difficulties," including the need for load leveling, improved citations, less "blind" requesting, and compliance with copyright law.[10]

### *Cooperation and Consortia*

The earliest cooperative efforts in the United States focused on the shared cataloging of books and serials. A major advancement in verification and location of serials, the *Union List of Serials in Libraries in the United States and Canada*, was published in 1927, under the auspices of the Library of Congress.

Regional cooperation also blossomed in the United States, facilitating ILL both directly and indirectly with programs such as shared cataloging and centralized storage or cooperative acquisitions or both. Some of the earliest regional cooperatives that continue today include the Bibliographical Center for Research (BCR), founded in 1935 in the western United States; the New England Depository Library (NEDL), which opened in 1942; and the Center for Research Libraries (CRL), which began as the Midwest Inter-Library Center in 1949.

### *Technology*

The technology developed in the 1900s continued to build on that of the previous century. In the 1920s Bell Labs developed a forerunner to the modern telefacsimile (fax) machine. During the 1930s Kodak's Recordak Division began microfilming newspapers, such as the *New York Times*, as concern for preservation began to grow. From 1941 to 1945, amid the bombing and destruction of World War II, a realization dawned that microfilm could also preserve other records of civilization, such as documents found in the archives and libraries of various countries. In 1935, telex machines, using telephone-like rotary dialing to connect teletype machines, were put into use, functionally automating message routing.

In 1946 the ENIAC (Electronic Numerical Integrator and Computer), the first electronic computer, was developed for the U.S. Army. The public had little idea of the impact this invention would have in the future.

*Copyright*

A major revision of the U.S. Copyright Act was completed in 1909, mostly concerned with broadening the scope of categories protected and extending the term of protection. Interlibrary loan activity in the United States was still considered moderate and therefore was not a focus of this revision. Another revision came in 1947; again ILL practices were not affected.

## 1950–1969

*Codes*

As postwar research and student populations continued to grow, so did interlibrary loan and the need for further revision of the ILL Code. The *General Interlibrary Loan Code of 1952* was even longer and more defensive than its predecessors. It explicitly sought to establish "standard procedures to cut costs and control the greatly increased volume of loans . . . and to relieve a measure of the present strain on the large research libraries which bear the principal burden of the loans between libraries." Notably, the primary purpose of interlibrary loan became to make library materials "available for research and for serious study" with no reference to the needs of the average reader, and two weeks, not four, was suggested as a reasonable loan period.[11]

Perhaps the most important feature of the 1952 code was the introduction of the first standardized ILL request form. It was a half-sheet, four-part carbon form designed for window envelopes. The multipart form enabled libraries to more easily notify each other by mail regarding shipment and return of requested items and to request renewals.[12] This form, with minor modifications, was used over the next few decades to request material. It was also the basis for the ALA ILL Request form that remains a part of the ILL code today.

In part in response to improved, though mostly still printed, tools for verification and location of library materials, the *National Interlibrary Loan Code, 1968* had a less defensive tone than its immediate predecessors. In a major change, this code, for the first time, was accompanied by a *Model Interlibrary Loan Code for Regional, State, Local or Other Special Groups of Libraries.* The Model Code was intended to be modified and adopted, as needed, by groups of libraries below the national level, which had begun to play a more significant role in ILL and resource sharing during this period.[13]

*Cooperation and Consortia*

In 1956, a major initiative of the Library of Congress and libraries across the country bore fruit: the first volumes of the *National Union Catalog of Pre-1956 Imprints* were published, containing invaluable bibliographic and location information. This and other printed tools for verifying and locating books and serials helped overcome two of the major barriers to effective interlibrary loan—knowing exactly what was needed and where it was located—and fueled the growth of ILL well into the 1970s. In addition to cooperative cataloging efforts at the national level, more libraries and related institutions began coming together at the local, state, and regional levels to deal with ongoing challenges, including the rising cost of acquisitions, interlibrary loan, collection storage, and related emerging technologies. Two of the more familiar names among the cooperatives originating during this period are the Committee on Institutional Cooperation (CIC), founded in 1957, in the Midwest, and the New England Library and Information Network (NELINET), founded in 1966.

In 1966, as computers were just beginning to impact libraries, the Library Services and Construction Act (LSCA), Title III, became law to support multitype library cooperatives. In what was to become a watershed development, the first incarnation of OCLC, then known as the Ohio College Library Center, was founded in 1967 as a nonprofit membership organization to foster computerized access to information, to facilitate resource sharing, and to reduce library costs.

### *Technology*

In the 1950s, interest in microfilming for the preservation of rare and unique material in libraries continued. In addition to film, microcards, microprint, and later microfiche were also being used. Computing continued to develop as an expensive and esoteric field. In 1951 the UNIVAC (Universal Automatic Computer), the first general-purpose commercial computer, was developed and delivered to the U.S. Census Bureau. The National Cash Register Company (NCR) developed carbonless paper in 1954 as a "less messy" replacement for carbon paper. Library supply companies subsequently adopted carbonless paper for use in the new four-part, ALA-approved ILL form.

The 1960s saw many innovations that had far-reaching effects on interlibrary loan workflow. In March of 1960, Haloid Xerox shipped the first plain-paper copier to a paying customer. Libraries quickly adopted photocopiers, which opened whole new vistas for ILL. The IBM Selectric electronic typewriter appeared in 1961, featuring several programmable keys. These keys enabled ILL offices to reduce the number of keystrokes needed to complete the four-part paper ILL request forms. Bell System–approved modems came into use in the 1960s to connect computers by phone lines. In the late 1960s, e-mail was developed for the Multics mainframe operating system, and the U.S. Department of Defense began test operations using ARPANET (the Advanced Research Projects Agency Network), forerunner to the Internet. These two developments eventually made e-mail between any two computers possible. Much as before, people generally regarded these innovations as interesting curiosities, having nothing to do with daily life in the United States.

By 1969 the Library of Congress had begun advocating use of its MARC format. Assigning fields to bibliographic records made standardized library computing and improved resource sharing possible in the years to come.

### *Copyright*

The United States began participating in the Geneva Universal Copyright Convention (UCC) in 1955. The UCC was designed as an alternative to the Berne Convention and allowed the United States to participate in some form of multilateral copyright protection without a major overhaul of U.S. copyright law. By the late 1960s, however, the escalating debate between libraries and rights holders, especially publishers of periodicals, concerning the impact of photocopy machines in libraries indicated that a major reworking of U.S. copyright law was inevitable.

## THE REVOLUTION BEGINS: ILL IN THE UNITED STATES, 1970–1999

During the 1970s, a technological revolution began that continues to transform the creation, management, and dissemination of information throughout the world today. As previously indicated, the proliferation of consortia proved to be both product and producer of advancements. This was especially true from 1970 onward. Advances in ILL stopped fitting into the relatively neat categories of the "evolutionary" period. Technological advances spurred changes in ILL codes, consortial activity often drove technology forward, and copyright issues loomed over the library landscape.

### Codes

Changes occurred so rapidly during this period that not only were the ALA ILL Code and forms revised several times but other guidelines were also adopted to address changing technologies and changing attitudes concerning ILL.

The ALA ILL form was revised in 1977. In 1980 revisions of the National ILL Code and Model Code were approved, and both codes remained integral parts of the U.S. resource-sharing landscape until the "National Interlibrary Loan Code for the United States, 1993" was approved. This code was published with the 1988 revisions to the ALA ILL form but without a Model Code. The 1993 code was much more access-oriented than its predecessors and was itself seen as an appropriate model for consortia and other groups of libraries as well as for the country at large.[14]

The growing use of fax technology for the delivery of requests and articles led to the need for guidelines. The year 1990 saw the adoption of Guidelines and Procedures for Telefacsimile Transmission of Interlibrary Loan Requests. As delivery shifted to Internet transmission of documents, a revised version was approved in 1994 as Guidelines and Procedures for Telefacsimile and Electronic Delivery of Interlibrary Loan Requests and Materials. Once electronic delivery of ILL requests and materials became the norm, these separate guidelines were withdrawn in favor of related revisions to the Explanatory Supplement to the U.S. ILL code.

In 1994 the first Guidelines for the Loan of Rare and Unique Materials were approved to encourage lending from formerly "off-limits" special library collections.

### Cooperation and Consortia

Not surprisingly, libraries and library organizations played a major role in the ILL revolution from its earliest days, to the great benefit of resource sharing in general and interlibrary loan in particular. Beginning in the mid-1970s, the National Commission on Libraries and Information Science (NCLIS), among other entities, led a concerted effort to develop a unified national network for library and information services. One goal of the commission was to provide everyone in the United States access to the information resources they needed. The network did not come to fruition as originally conceived, and, over time, the concept of a single national network evolved into a network of networks that continues today. Along the way, a new kind of library organization was born—the bibliographic utility—an entity that facilitates the development of bibliographic databases and offers related products and services such as union catalogs, authority control, collection assessment tools, interlibrary loan systems, or any combination of these. OCLC became the first and largest, but not the only, such organization to make significant contributions to the ongoing revolution in library services.

In 1974 three Ivy League universities and the New York Public Library formed the Research Libraries Group (RLG) to meet the specialized needs of research libraries and their users. Also in 1974 the Washington Library Network was formed in the Pacific Northwest, later to become the Western Library Network (WLN). In 1977 OCLC became the Online Computer Library Center and began to expand its membership and systems beyond Ohio via regional networks.

In the early 1980s, RLG expanded membership to include key research libraries across the United States and introduced the Research Libraries Information Network (RLIN) shared cataloging and ILL systems. Also, the WLN system, particularly noted for its authority control and collection assessment components, continued to expand its reach within the United States and beyond, including Australia. By 1992 RLG membership comprised more than one hundred North American and overseas members, including the British Library. The Western Library Network merged with OCLC in 1999, and its online catalog and other offerings were incorporated into OCLC services such as WorldCat.

Concurrent with the rise of bibliographic utilities in the United States, the Z39.50 standard and the ISO ILL Protocol were developed to enable the peer-to-peer exchange of information between different online catalogs and ILL systems, respectively. Although Z39.50 has been widely adopted throughout the world for catalog searching, the ISO ILL Protocol, developed in Canada, is used much more sparingly in the United States than in Canada or Europe.

## Technology

In the 1970s companies began to develop modems outside strict Bell System approval; these modems, encased in a briefcase-sized carrier, connected computers through phone lines by clamping acoustic couplers over the mouth- and earpieces of the telephone.

The Bell System began marketing the Teletypewriter Exchange (TWX) machine to transfer data. Libraries such as CRL began accepting TWX orders. To cut telecommunications costs, requesters used a keyboard to punch a paper-tape offline, creating the ILL request. The tape was then run through the machine online to send the request.

By the mid-1970s microform technology had grown in popularity with better quality film and improved readers and reader-printers. Libraries began producing and distributing COM (Computer Output Microform) catalogs in the form of microfiche sets, making their holdings more widely available. ILL offices used multiple COM catalogs, checking individual libraries for holdings.

In 1971 OCLC initiated the first shared online library cataloging system, which had multiple holdings on one record and eventually made COM catalogs obsolete. By 1979 OCLC began production of its ILL Service, linking request forms to both bibliographic and holdings information.

By the mid-1970s companies such as Lexis, BRS, and DIALOG were providing hundreds of citation databases. The ease of searching a single database versus the tedium of searching multiple annual volumes for bibliographic citations greatly increased the number of ILL requests made each year.

In the late 1970s a new generation of smaller fax machines became ubiquitous, offering faster, more efficient, and cheaper service. Patrons and ILL staff alike realized that these machines could deliver articles faster than the U.S. mail.

In 1981 Hayes Microcomputer Products introduced the Smartmodem, containing a controller that sent commands to the computer and enabled it to operate the phone line. This kind of technology remains the basis for online communication today. Database providers such as DIALOG and BRS began offering special subsets of their search services such as BRS Afterdark, which allowed users to do their own database searching at considerable cost savings. Ease of connection, cheaper phone rates, and the enormity of data available allowed users to harvest numerous bibliographic citations, and ILL requests skyrocketed.

In 1986 OCLC developed the ILL Microenhancer (ILLME) to help ILL practitioners update their growing batches of requests more effectively. The ILLME enabled staff members to mark records offline for updating and later upload them into the OCLC ILL subsystem.

ILL practitioners recognized the need for management systems to help cope with various aspects of ILL. During the 1990s a progression of software was developed to automate and streamline the ILL process. In 1991 SAVEIT (the System for Automating Vital Elements of Interlibrary Transactions) was developed to assist with record keeping and statistics. It was supplanted by Clio, a more sophisticated system developed by Perkins and Associates in 1996. ILLiad was developed by Atlas Systems for Virginia Tech and launched in 1999. The following year OCLC began distributing ILLiad as a complement to the OCLC WorldCat Resource Sharing system.

Other major developments involved tools to aid in the delivery of copies. In 1991 RLG released Ariel, which uses a scanner and the Internet, rather than fax technology, for document delivery.

### Copyright

Although technological advances made information sharing easier and faster, they also caused rights holders more and more alarm. As early as 1973 lawsuits such as *Williams and Wilkins Co. v. United States* occurred, focusing on the making of unauthorized photocopies of articles. Widespread adoption of photocopy machines in libraries, especially in ILL, was a major reason that the U.S. Congress passed the Copyright Act of 1976. Although Sections 107 and 108 of the new law included provisions relevant to ILL photocopying, they caused considerable confusion in libraries. Later in 1976 the National Commission on New Technological Uses of Copyrighted Works (CONTU) attempted to clarify matters by issuing guidelines. Both the 1976 Act and the "CONTU Guidelines" are still in effect and still sometimes cause confusion, especially among new ILL practitioners. In fact, the 1976 Act is *law* and the CONTU Guidelines are *not*. The 1976 Act also triggered concern on the part of ILL departments regarding record keeping and the payment of royalties. In 1978 the Copyright Clearance Center (CCC) was established by authors and publishers to act as a clearinghouse for royalty fees.

In 1988 the United States signed the Berne Convention, resulting in the elimination of the requirement for copyright notice. By the early 1990s, rapid development of the Internet allowed information sharing in ways that the Copyright Act of 1976 could not imagine. The result was the 1998 Digital Millennium Copyright Act (DMCA), which attempts to address online infringement of copyright.

### Other Developments

The latter part of the twentieth century also saw revolutionary developments in other aspects of ILL practice: the proliferation of publications specifically addressed to ILL practitioners, an increase in cost and performance studies aimed exclusively at ILL, and the creation of new service alternatives.

*Dedicated Publications*

Accompanying the explosion of ILL activity, publications began to appear specializing in aiding practitioners with how-to's and giving them a platform to share best practices. Among the how-to's, Sarah Katharine Thomson's *Interlibrary Loan Procedure Manual* was published by ALA in 1970, largely in response to ALA approval of the 1968 ILL and Model Codes. The development and rapid acceptance of online ILL systems soon made the need for a new manual necessary. In 1984, ALA published Virginia Boucher's *Interlibrary Loan Practices Handbook,* followed by a second edition in 1997.

Virginia Boucher also was responsible for an early ILL newsletter. Bearing the catchy title *just b'twx us,* it was produced at the University of Colorado and ran sporadically from 1970 to 1986. In 1988, Mary Jackson's bimonthly "Library to Library" column began its run in the *Wilson Library Bulletin.* By 1990 Haworth Press began publication of a full-fledged periodical dedicated to ILL, the *Journal of Interlibrary Loan and Information Supply,* edited by Leslie R. Morris.

Methods of communicating among ILL practitioners have evolved along with the Internet. In the 1980s electronic discussion lists began popping up to help ILL practitioners connect to one another. One of the earliest discussion lists that is still going strong is ILL-L. As the Internet has become even more sophisticated, ILL practitioners have adopted wikis, blogs, and other new technologies for information sharing.

*Cost and Performance Studies*

With the proliferation of ILL activity during the 1990s, libraries were faced with several questions: Does it cost less or more to provide material through ILL than to purchase a needed book or article? What are the hidden costs of ILL? How can libraries determine where to spend money to achieve less staff stress, faster turnaround, and greater patron satisfaction? Cost and performance studies began in earnest during this period. Among the more comprehensive studies were two involving Association of Research Libraries (ARL) institutions: *The ARL/RLG Interlibrary Loan Cost Study,* published in 1993, followed by *Measuring the Performance of ILL Operations in North American Research and College Libraries* in 1998. In 2004 ARL published *Assessing ILL/DD Services: New Cost-Effective Alternatives.* In addition to providing cost and other data from research and some college libraries, these studies identified several ILL and document delivery best practices that are of value to all types of libraries.

*New Resource-Sharing Models*

By the mid-1990s, some consortia began to offer a new type of resource sharing, featuring direct patron-initiated requesting of books from other libraries. This alternative to traditional ILL employs software that enables institutions to share user status and item-availability information. One example is OhioLink, which began full production in 1996. This new service model introduced new practices and procedures and sparked a need for codes to govern them. Consortia often adapted existing ILL codes to address the needs of the new resource-sharing environment.

## THE TWENTY-FIRST CENTURY

Developments in the twenty-first century will seem mild in comparison to the profound impact of technology on resource sharing that occurred in the twentieth century. Nonetheless, enhancements in technology continue to impact the practice of resource sharing and have allowed ILL units the ability to improve and expand services as well as focus on developing relationships with other libraries.

### Codes

ALA's Reference and User Services Association (RUSA) now requires reviews of its codes and guidelines every seven years. Therefore, we've seen two revisions of the U.S. ILL code since 1993. The first was a major overhaul of the code in 2001, incorporating references to unmediated ILL and redefining the date due of an ILL item as the date the item is due back at the lending library. Another major change in 2001 was to the two-part format that we have today: (1) the *Interlibrary Loan Code for the United States,* itself, containing the essential and relatively "timeless" guidelines for interlibrary borrowing and lending,[15] accompanied by (2) the *Explanatory Supplement for Use with the Interlibrary Loan Code for the United States,* which amplifies the provisions of the code and provides "fuller explanation and specific examples for text that is intentionally general and prescriptive."[16] This format was adopted so that the more general code, which requires formal approval by RUSA, would need less-frequent revision while the detailed Explanatory Supplement could easily be revised as needed.

Interlibrary borrowing and lending in the United States today are conducted under an ILL Code and Explanatory Supplement that were revised in 2008. As expected, the 2008 revisions to the code were very minor while a few substantive changes were made to the Explanatory Supplement to address such current issues as discouraging the use of adhesive labels on borrowed items and the need to request special uses of items in advance.

Among other codes, revised Guidelines for the Interlibrary Loan of Rare and Unique Material were approved in 2004. Approval of another revision is expected in 2011.

### Cooperation and Consortia

One of the most intense, if short-lived, uses of both Z39.50 and the ISO ILL Protocol involving U.S. libraries began in 2000, when RLG introduced ILL Manager, a peer-to-peer ILL management system. In 2003 RLG migrated all of its consortial ILL activity to peer-to-peer systems like ILL Manager and retired the RLIN ILL system.

In 2006, however, RLG combined with OCLC, the RLIN Union Catalog was merged into OCLC WorldCat, RLG's citation databases moved to OCLC FirstSearch, and RLG ILL activity moved to OCLC WorldCat Resource Sharing and ILLiad. Today, OCLC serves more than 72,000 libraries of all types in the United States and over 170 countries and territories around the world. OCLC is closer than ever to being a de facto national network for the United States and has an increasing international scope as well.

### Technology

After a flood destroyed most of its periodical collection in 1997, Colorado State University developed FastFlood software to expedite the delivery of journal articles. In 2001, this service evolved into RapidILL and since has become international in scope.

Article delivery methods are also changing: electronic journal providers are becoming more inclined to allow direct delivery of PDF files, eliminating the need for ILL staff to go through multiple conversions between electronic and paper formats. In 2003, Atlas Systems introduced its Internet document transmission software, Odyssey, which can function either as part of ILLiad or as a stand-alone product.

Delivery of materials is also changing in the formerly highly restrictive area of academic dissertations and theses. Institutions are adopting the practice of accepting and providing direct access to their theses and dissertations in electronic format only (ETDs). ProQuest's Dissertation and Theses database, the successor to *Dissertation Abstracts,* also offers a full-text option for many theses. These academic works, once so carefully guarded in the library's archives and often unavailable for ILL, are now much more freely available.

## INTERNATIONAL LIBRARY COOPERATION

Changing technology continues to blur the boundaries of ILL among countries on all continents. The International Federation of Library Associations and Institutions (IFLA) plays a major role in facilitating library activity among countries. As early as 1927, librarianship as a profession had solidified around the world to the point that IFLA was founded in Scotland as the global voice of the library and information profession. Within its first ten years, IFLA worked out a system of international library loans, even proposing in 1932 that international loans be a principal theme of its Second World Congress held in Madrid in 1935. A duty-free loan system and uniform rules and procedures among participating libraries were proposed. By the Warsaw meeting in 1936, nineteen countries had joined the plan, which was unfortunately interrupted by World War II in 1939.

By the mid-1950s, IFLA resumed a strong role in facilitating communications among libraries worldwide, approving its *International Lending and Document Delivery: Principles and Guidelines for Procedure* in 1954. Subsequently, international ILL became a necessity rather than a luxury for researchers and prompted three revisions of the principles and guidelines between 1978 and 2001. In the late 1970s, IFLA established a Core Programme for Universal Availability of Publications and an Office for International Lending. Today, the Document Delivery and Resource Sharing Section encourages libraries throughout the world to make information in all formats available using a variety of resource-sharing and document supply techniques. The section monitors international resource-sharing developments and provides information through its website, a semiannual newsletter, interlending conferences, document delivery workshops, and cooperative projects with other international organizations. In 1995 IFLA introduced its Voucher Scheme, which enables libraries to pay for ILL transactions with reusable vouchers, negating the need for invoices, bank transfers, and currency conversions, further facilitating international lending transactions. Today IFLA has over 1,600 member libraries in approximately 150 countries worldwide.

## CONCLUSION

As we move into the second decade of the twenty-first century, many issues in interlibrary loan continue to evolve: staff and delivery costs; copyright versus contract law; the sharing of international, electronic, or rare and unique materials; the communication of policies; and even the locus of ILL in the library. Also, both bibliographic utilities and regional networks are transforming themselves in response to a rapidly changing environment. An example is the 2009 emergence of Lyrasis, formed by the joining of SOLINET, PALINET, and NELINET. As in the past, we in interlibrary loan will meet the challenges of continuing technological, legal, organizational, and societal changes. One thing is constant: we interlibrary loan practitioners will continue to do our best to connect users with the information they desire, regardless of its format or location.

## NOTES

1. Roy MacLeod, "Introduction: Alexandria in History and Myth," in *The Library of Alexandria: Centre of Learning in the Ancient World,* edited by Roy MacLeod (London: I. B. Tauris, 2000), 4–5.
2. Karl Christ, *The Handbook of Medieval Library History,* trans. Theophil M. Otto (Metuchen, NJ: Scarecrow Press, 1984), 113.
3. William H. Carlson, "Cooperation: An Historical Review and a Forecast," *College and Research Libraries* 13, no. 1 (1951): 5.
4. Samuel S. Green, "The Lending of Books to One Another by Libraries," *American Library Journal* 1, no. 1 (1876): 15–16.
5. Samuel S. Green, "Interlibrary Loans in Reference Work," *Library Journal* 23, no. 2 (1898): 567–68.
6. Ibid., 568.
7. Elizabeth W. Stone, *American Library Development, 1600–1899* (New York: H. W. Wilson, 1977), 287.
8. C. H. Gould, "[Report of the ALA] Committee on Co-ordination [regarding the *Code of Practice for Interlibrary Loans*]," *Library Journal* 42 (1917): 634.
9. Ibid.
10. "Interlibrary Loan Code–1940," *College and Research Libraries* 3 (September 1941): 318–19, 376.
11. "General Interlibrary Loan Code, 1952," *College and Research Libraries* 13, no. 4 (October 1952): 350–55.
12. Ibid., Appendix II, 355–58.
13. Sarah Katharine Thomson, "Model Interlibrary Loan Code for Regional, State, Local or Other Special Groups of Libraries, Annotated," *Interlibrary Loan Procedure Manual* (Chicago: American Library Association, 1970), 8–17.
14. Reference and User Services Association, "National Interlibrary Loan Code for the United States, 1993," *RQ* 33, no. 4 (Summer 1994): 477–79.
15. Reference and User Services Association, "Interlibrary Loan Code for the United States," *Reference and User Services Quarterly* 40, no. 4 (Summer 2001): 318–19.
16. Reference and User Services Association, "Explanatory Supplement for Use with the Interlibrary Loan Code for the United States," *Reference and User Services Quarterly* 40, no. 4 (Summer 2001): 312–27.

## BIBLIOGRAPHY

Carlson, William H. "Cooperation: An Historical Review and a Forecast." *College and Research Libraries* 13, no. 1 (1951): 5–13.

Christ, Karl. *The Handbook of Medieval Library History.* Translated by Theophil M. Otto. Metuchen, NJ: Scarecrow Press, 1984.

"General Interlibrary Loan Code, 1952." *College and Research Libraries* 13, no. 4 (October 1952): 350–58.

Gould, C. H. "[Report of the ALA] Committee on Co-ordination [regarding the *Code of Practice for Interlibrary Loans*]." *Library Journal* 42 (1917): 634–35.

Green, Samuel S. "The Lending of Books to One Another by Libraries." *American Library Journal* 1, no. 1 (1876): 15–16.

———. "Interlibrary Loans in Reference Work," *Library Journal* 23, no. 2 (1898): 567–68.

"Interlibrary Loan Code–1940," *College and Research Libraries* 3 (September 1941): 318–19, 376.

MacLeod, Roy. "Introduction: Alexandria in History and Myth." In *The Library of Alexandria: Centre of Learning in the Ancient World,* edited by Roy MacLeod. London: I. B. Tauris, 2000, 1–15.

Reference and User Services Association. "Explanatory Supplement for Use with the Interlibrary Loan Code for the United States." *Reference and User Services Quarterly* 40, no. 4 (Summer 2001): 321–27.

Reference and User Services Association. "Interlibrary Loan Code for the United States." *Reference and User Services Quarterly* 40, no. 4 (Summer 2001): 318–19.

Reference and User Services Association. "National Interlibrary Loan Code for the United States, 1993." *RQ* 33, no. 4 (Summer 1994): 477–79.

Stone, Elizabeth W. *American Library Development, 1600–1899.* New York: H. W. Wilson, 1977.

Thomson, Sarah Katharine. "Model Interlibrary Loan Code for Regional, State, Local, or Other Special Groups of Libraries, Annotated." In *Interlibrary Loan Procedure Manual.* Chicago: American Library Association, 1970.

CHAPTER TWO

# BORROWING WORKFLOW BASICS

*Denise Forro*

IN AN AGE when it seems as if everything a patron needs can be found on the Internet, the reality is that she discovers more references to materials that are of interest but is unable to access the content online. The user then turns to the interlibrary loan office for assistance in gaining access to this material. Additionally, libraries are finding that it is often more cost-effective to provide access to materials through ILL services instead of purchasing the items for their collections. Consequently, borrowing items for the patron is still a vital service for the library. Anecdotally, libraries are experiencing an increase in ILL request volume. What many practitioners are experiencing is borne out in one survey of eighty-six academic libraries in which the mean aggregate request volume increased by over 21 percent from 2005 to 2008.[1] Given these numbers, it is important that all libraries operate their interlibrary loan unit efficiently and effectively to better serve their patrons' needs.

## BORROWING POLICIES

It is critical to develop policies for interlibrary loan so that patrons and staff members are confident in how to proceed. This groundwork enables good patron-staff relationships and expedites fulfillment of requested materials. Many of the software programs used for ILL management will assist with following those procedures. For libraries that do not use a management program, it is an inherent responsibility of the staff to be aware of these policies. Making sure that patrons and other library staff are informed about the policies and posting them in appropriate places will eliminate many unnecessary questions about the service. Most libraries post their policies on their library website, although print brochures and handouts may be used.

At the most basic level, the policy should include information about who is allowed to request, what may be requested, how you will communicate with the requesting patron, the method by which items are to be delivered to the patron and in what average time frame, and the cost of the service. Patrons also need to know about loan periods and renewals, how materials are to be returned, and any policies regarding lost or damaged items.

A more detailed discussion of policies can be found in chapter 5, "Management of Interlibrary Loan." However, several elements may be overlooked that can cause difficulties for the library staff and confusion or frustration for patrons. If the library is unable to support unlimited requesting, patrons must know how many requests may be submitted. Fees should also be addressed in the policy statement as patrons may be unwilling or unable to pay fees associated with their requests. Along with the amount charged for the service, patrons need to know the process for payment. Your policy should specify whether fees should be paid up front, before the request is processed, or after receipt. If there is no charge, indicate that to avoid confusion later. Many academic libraries do not charge for their services but do alert the patron about the cost of the service to the institution. Sometimes, the service is free to the patron unless a copyright royalty must be paid. In this case, the patron should be contacted before the request is placed so that he is aware of the potential charge. Copyright is covered in depth in chapter 4.

A patron's physical location can sometimes determine if she is eligible to receive interlibrary loan services. In the case of a public library, the patron may be required to live in a certain area to receive this service. At one time, interlibrary loan and document delivery for academic libraries would have been limited to faculty, students, and staff members who were on campus. In today's world of online learning, however, many of these libraries have extended ILL service to those involved in distance learning programs and to online students. A library may offer additional services for distance education students that it might not provide to local patrons, such as sending books directly to the individual and scanning documents from print sources. It is important to communicate these service options to patrons involved in distance education programs, either through a website or brochure.

Twenty years ago, the process of loaning materials between libraries was so labor intensive and took such a long time that interlibrary loan was discouraged as a service to all but the most intense researchers or those willing to pay. Today, patrons expect and can receive quick turnaround times for the materials they request. Policies should note time expectations for the receipt of patron materials. In an era of almost instant satisfaction, interlibrary loan may seem slow, so realistic expectations are necessary for an effective service.

Policy statements should also suggest to patrons when to consider placing an interlibrary loan request and when to seek other assistance such as additional help from a reference desk. Although many practitioners feel that ILL should not be used in lieu of purchasing materials, it is appropriate for libraries to delineate what is permissible. Over time, some of the thinking in this area has changed. In earlier editions of this handbook, a philosophy of interlibrary loan as a last resort was suggested: "Full use of the library's collection should be made before interlibrary borrowing is attempted (the Code, 2.1)."[2] As noted by Boucher, this guideline is stated in the Interlibrary Loan Code for the United States, but fewer libraries adhere to this policy now than in the past. If the material is in the collection but currently checked out, it may make more sense to request a loan from another library than to recall the item from the patron who is currently using it. In many cases, interlibrary loan is faster than a recall process that can take weeks to complete. Items may also be locally available, but not in a desired format or available for checkout, such as books in a reference or reserve collection. Whether these materials are eligible for request through interlibrary loan or not is also a local policy decision.

## REQUEST FORMS

Patrons need or want to access many items. These materials come in many forms and formats. The borrowing unit should have as much correct information as possible to locate a possible lender and successfully fill the request for the patron.

Request forms, whether online or in print, are based on the Interlibrary Loan Data Elements of the NISO ILL standard and found in the ALA Interlibrary Loan Request Form (see chapter appendixes 2.1 and 2.2).[3] This form is multipurpose for requesting different types of material. The elements found on the form are universally used by the many systems that exist to process requests and are easily recognizable by lending libraries. In a perfect world, users would submit request forms on which they have completed every field with accurate and complete information. In reality, users may not know or understand every bibliographic element about the item they are requesting, and library staff may not need every data element in order to locate the requested item and identify lenders. However, it is best practice to include the bibliographic elements shown in figure 2.1 on a request form if users have this level of detail or require it to describe the item they are requesting.

Additional elements of information can be helpful for library staff to manage borrowing requests. In some cases, having the citation's source assists staff with difficult requests that may need to be tracked back to their origin. Today, because of the Internet, it is not as crucial to the success of the request to have this information, but it can be beneficial for materials that are difficult to obtain. Patrons should also include a "need by" date. This is a date after which the delivery of the item would no longer be useful. If your library allows a choice of method for delivery, this must also be noted. Patrons may have a preference for online rather than mail delivery of articles if there is a choice. In submitting a request, the patron must acknowledge any fees or copyright charges that he is expected to pay. This acknowledgment should be made through online billing or indicated in some other way. If payment is expected when placing the request, patrons must know this, and the library must have a method for accepting and acknowledging payment.

Patrons requesting numerous items at one time should be made aware that other patrons are also requesting materials and that they might need to prioritize their requests if a quota system is in place. If the borrowing process is automated with online forms, such prioritizing is not quite as critical unless the requests are mediated. Here again, the library may want to clearly state this in its policies. Finally, the most important item on a request form is one required by law: a copyright notice. See chapter 4 for a detailed discussion of the requirements of Title 17, Section 108 of the U.S. Code.

## THE DISCOVERY PROCESS AND TOOLS

Before the advent of computerized bibliographic utilities and the use of the Internet as a discovery tool, locating lenders for requested items was labor intensive.

**Figure 2.1** Types of Material Requested and Basic Elements Needed to Locate a Lender

| Data Element | Book Loans | Article | Dissertation | Microforms | Media | Conference Proceedings | Newspapers | Government Documents |
|---|---|---|---|---|---|---|---|---|
| Author | X | | X | X | | | | X |
| Title | X | | X | X | X | X | X | X |
| Edition | X | | | | | | | |
| Publisher | X | | | X | | | | |
| Place of Publication | X | X | X | | | | X | |
| Date of Publication (Year) | X | X | X | X | X | X | X | X |
| Series Title | X | | | X | | | | |
| Article Author | | X | | | | | X | |
| Article Title | | X | | | | | X | |
| Journal Title | | X | | | | | | |
| Volume Number | | X | | | | | | |
| Issue Number | | X | | | | | X | |
| Issue Date | | X | | | | | X | |
| Page Numbers | | X | | | | | X | |
| Degree-granting Institution | | | X | | | | | |
| Degree Granted | | | X | | | | | |
| Artists, Actors, Directors | | | | | X | | | |
| Studio or Producer | | | | | X | | | |
| Name of Conference | | | | | | X | | |
| Conference Location/Sponsor | | | | | | X | | |
| Government Agency/Body | | | | | | | | X |
| SuDoc Number | | | | | | | | X |

Today, many avenues are available to locate the materials and potential lending libraries. Staff members who are processing requests can go to national utilities, web search engines, online catalogs, or interlibrary loan e-mail lists.

## National Utilities

Perhaps the most well-known utility with easy web access is OCLC WorldCat. This database consists of bibliographic records entered into the system by libraries around the world in conjunction with acquisition and cataloging processes. As a library catalogs a new bibliographic record in the system, it attaches its unique OCLC symbol to that record. As other member libraries acquire the same item, they also attach their library's symbol to the record. This process makes it fairly easy to determine if a particular library has a given item. Patrons are also able to search this database through WorldCat.org on the Web. The interlibrary loan subsystem of OCLC is the WorldCat Resource Sharing (WCRS) network and is frequently accessed through OCLC FirstSearch or an ILL management system.

PubMed (www.ncbi.nlm.nih.gov/pubmed/) is a national service that includes citations from Medline covering medicine and the health sciences and is supported by the National Library of Medicine. PubMed is an online interface that is available to everyone, while the more comprehensive database, Medline, is only available if the library subscribes through a commercial database vendor.

### Online Catalogs

Most libraries today have online catalogs that are available through the Web and open to the public for searching. These catalogs give you access not only to the bibliographic data but also to the current status of the material in the library. The difficulty with this method for locating items is the piecemeal searching it requires. However, if the library is part of a group, if you need to stay within a specific region, if you suspect a particular library may have the material, or if you are in a rush and want to request only material shown to be available, then online catalogs are certainly an option.

### Additional Resources

Various search engines on the Web facilitate searching for materials. Google Books and Google Scholar are two examples of specialized web search engines that assist with the discovery process. In the case of difficult-to-locate items, these tools may be paramount to finding a possible lender.

Archival collections are typically very difficult to borrow, but increasingly libraries will be able to digitize materials on request. A variety of sources exist that can assist in locating the holder of an archival or manuscript collection. In addition to a general web search or a search of WorldCat, Archive Finder is a subscription database of archival collections. A free resource that may assist is the National Union Catalog of Manuscript Collections (NUCMC), available at www.loc.gov/coll/nucmc/.

Finally, as a last resort, staff can turn to the various online or e-mail discussion lists that support interlibrary loan. If you have trouble locating a citation, another ILL librarian may be able to find the record that you need.

## REQUEST SYSTEMS

After a patron submits a request, library staff must then locate the requested item, identify holding libraries, and submit the request. The act of placing a request with a lending library typically happens on one of the major interlibrary loan systems in use. Many systems allow for requests to be placed with multiple potential lenders. This option allows the request to pass from one potential lender to the next in a queue without having to be returned to the borrowing library each time a lender is unable to supply. Library staff members should determine whether the lenders they are querying have a borrowing fee or whether a reciprocal arrangement exists with the lending library. Many libraries cooperate in a consortium and offer free service to one another. If this is not the case, then the library will need to make arrangements for payment, which may also occur within the request system being used or outside the system through an invoice.

### Direct Consortial Borrowing

Direct Consortial Borrowing systems unite information in either a single union catalog or a virtual searching and linking that allows requesting of certain types of materials. Often these systems are based on the circulation system of the library or, in the case of article requesting, based on the serial holdings of the participant libraries. Patron direct requesting is possible through these systems, making it unnecessary for staff to mediate the requests at the time they are placed. Physical processing of the materials is usually the same as other incoming filled requests. Some of these systems work in conjunction with interlibrary loan management systems, creating a central location for patron tracking of requests.

## REQUEST VERIFICATION AND PROBLEM RESOLUTION

It is overly simplistic to believe that all requests are easily found and that lending libraries are easily located for every item needed by patrons. On a daily basis, staff members will find that they must intercede, review requests for errors, and locate additional lending libraries when a request has been returned unfilled. This is where the training and knowledge of the library staff are most valuable. As Lee Andrew Hilyer memorably wrote, "Verification is both a skill and an art."[4]

In the past, when ILL was not as automated and when information was found only in print sources, the verification process was performed before the request was sent to potential lenders. In theory, patrons, now as then, are expected to supply the correct information, including a source. In practice, this is not necessarily the norm. Before the Internet, ILL staff would spend an inordinate amount of time tracking down the citation to verify its existence. In the online environment, where citation information is readily available through indexes, citation databases, utilities, and web browsers, this step does not have to be taken before the request is sent. If the citation is submitted by a patron through a database connection, it should already be complete and correct.

That being said, if lenders are unable to supply the material because of a poor or incomplete citation, then the ILL staff must verify that the item exists. Verification usually involves looking up the citation in the source that is given on the form. If a source is not given, staff may then consult various online and print subject indexes and abstracts. If this search fails to produce a confirmation of the citation, a reference librarian or subject specialist may be consulted. After using all these methods, ILL staff may need to either contact the patron and request more information or cancel the item with the indication that the citation could not be found and that the patron will need to identify the source for further investigation. Many times, patrons given this option do not respond. Either it is not worth the time to find the source, or the need has passed. Finally, if a patron insists that she needs a particular item and library staff cannot verify that it exists, ILL electronic discussion lists are great places to find assistance. Table 2.1 is a summary of common verification problems.

As with many aspects of research, there will be requests for which it is difficult if not impossible to find a lender. The citation may be so vague and the resource so unreliable that a straightforward search is not possible. Once you know that the citation has been represented correctly and the source is reputable, then you need to do an extensive search. The first step in the searching process is to consult bibliographic utilities to check for a record and possible lenders. There may be multiple records for the same title, so it is important to choose the record that has the most possible lenders. If one record does not result in a fill for a request, try one of the duplicate records.

**Table 2.1** Citation Verification Problems

| Common Problems Resolved through Citation Source, Index, Abstract, or the Web | Complex Problems Often Requiring Additional Work |
|---|---|
| • Abbreviations that cannot be identified<br>• Incomplete citations<br>• Incorrect spelling of author's name<br>• Incorrect volume, issue, page numbers, date, or year<br>• Multiple journals found with the same title | • Book requests that are actually book chapter requests<br>• Article requests that are actually books or book chapters<br>• Proceedings that have a separate title from the proceeding itself<br>• Monographic series that are classed separately or together<br>• Inability to locate a supplier for the format requested<br>• Numerous translations<br>• Duplicate bibliographic records found in bibliographic utility<br>• Punctuation within citation creating false return |

Occasionally a record will be found with no holding libraries. It is possible to send a request to the library that placed the record on the utility as a possible lender, though if that library is not indicated as a potential supplier, it could be an indication that the material has been lost or withdrawn. Once it is determined that the utility is an unproductive avenue, then staff should turn to international sources, like the British Library or other national libraries. Going to these libraries may mean registering with them and using the form particular to their institution. If the library participates in the International Federation of Library Associations and Institutions (IFLA), the International Loan/Photocopy Request Form (chapter appendix 2.2) is available. Some international libraries will accept e-mail requests or an ALA Interlibrary Loan Request form.

If it is simply not possible to find the title requested by the patron or if lenders are not willing to send the item, then it may be necessary to contact the patron about other possible editions and formats. A later edition may suffice, or, if not, a copy saved to microfilm or microfiche, although not the first choice of the patron, may provide the information needed.

## Resources

Bibliographic Utilities

- OCLC WorldCat
- PubMed (DOCLINE)

National and International Library Interlibrary Loan and Commercial Document Delivery Services

- British Library
- NRC Canada Institute for Scientific and Technical Information (NRC-CISTI)
- Webcat Plus (National Institute of Informatics)
- CAS (Chemical Abstracts Service)
- LHL Direct (Linda Hall Library, Document Services Department)

## SELECTING POTENTIAL LENDING LIBRARIES

For libraries who participate in WorldCat Resource Sharing (WCRS), it is common practice to create groups of preferred lenders, a process known as Custom Holdings. Though it is up to each library to establish its own criteria for grouping lenders, it is common to create groups based on format of material being requested, turnaround time as a lender, loan periods, consortial arrangements, geographic location, delivery method, and fees. Once a library has established Custom Holdings, it can use the Direct Request feature of WCRS to automate the requesting process. A more detailed discussion of both these processes is found in chapter 6.

You can request items from lenders located in specific time zones. For example, if it is late in the day on the East Coast, placing a request with a library on the West Coast may produce a faster turnaround time. Similarly, if it is late on the West Coast, placing the request with an East Coast library may prove faster. Another tip for faster turnaround times is to choose libraries that are less busy or that consistently supply quickly and accurately.

Many libraries have made arrangements through consortia or other groups to partner with them for optimal fulfillment of interlibrary loan requests and to share expenses. Reciprocal agreements can also be made individually between libraries. A letter of inquiry is sent to the library that is a potential match as a reciprocal partner. If the potential partner decides the relationship would be mutually beneficial, appropriate staff would sign and return the letter, keeping a copy for the institution's files. A group of libraries that agree to share without charging is the Libraries Very Interested in Sharing (LVIS) group. LVIS originated in Illinois and Missouri in 1993 and now includes over 2,600 participating libraries.[5] LVIS is particularly beneficial for smaller libraries, which have been able to obtain materials for their patrons without incurring higher costs.

However, such agreements do not obviate the necessity of going outside the group to find lenders for some items. Some libraries use commercial document delivery suppliers, especially if an article is needed urgently. These suppliers charge for their services, typically have a quick turnaround time, and usually add the copyright royalties to the cost of the transaction. This last feature eliminates the need for paying a copyright royalty later because it is paid up front; however, you may find that your use of the article falls under fair use and the copyright fee was paid unnecessarily. In other words, because the copyright fee is paid up front as a part of the document delivery service, it can be a trade-off—a higher cost for the item, but delivery of the article in a relatively short turnaround time. The library staff will need to determine when it is appropriate to obtain the material from a document delivery supplier.

## PURCHASE VERSUS BORROW

Patrons have developed expectations for immediate results because of their constant use of technology that responds instantaneously to their needs. This demand for a quick turnaround time for interlibrary loan and document delivery is a challenge for interlibrary loan operations. Many libraries have sought ways to reduce the time between the request and fulfillment of the item or the time to acquire recently published items. A purchase-on-demand program changes the nature of a request to a purchase that is supplied by a vendor or publisher that will provide the title quickly for the patron.

In the case of a book or other materials that would need to be returned, instead of borrowing a copy, the library may redirect a loan request from a lending library to a book dealer or publisher. The material may be new or used. It may be retained by the library as part of the collection, given to the patron to keep, or sold back to a vendor. The item in need may be sent to the library or directly to the patron. Either option is a current practice used by libraries with this type of service.

For articles, libraries may find that ordering directly from the publisher will result in very quick fulfillment of the request through online access, high user satisfaction, and lower fees overall. Purchasing directly from a publisher eliminates the need to pay copyright separately; however, the cost of the purchase may be higher than borrowing the material and paying copyright and should be reviewed for the best practice for the local institution.

A variety of procedural workflow options can be pursued when establishing a purchase-on-demand service, usually involving interlibrary loan, access services/circulation, acquisitions, cataloging, or any or all of these. A successful program will likely require communication and cooperation among these units. Libraries with this type of operation have found that patrons are satisfied with the quick response time, the almost immediate availability of the material, availability of requested articles online, and the quality of the item. If this type of situation is in place or being considered, policies and guidelines should be established to determine when to use this service and when to turn to regular interlibrary loan.

## RECEIVING MATERIALS

Borrowing units receive items in either print or electronic form. Physical materials arrive through various means, including postal services, commercial couriers, and consortial delivery systems. Copies may be delivered electronically through Ariel or Odyssey, transmitted in e-mail, posted to the Web, faxed, or sent through regular mail.

### Mailroom Practices

Physical items, whether books, media, microforms, or copies, will arrive in various types of packaging. These include envelopes, padded envelopes sometimes known as Jiffy bags, bubble wrap, media boxes, canvas bags, tubs or totes, and boxes. Even for small to medium-sized libraries, the volume can be surprising and take many staff hours each day to open and sort. When unpacking items, it is important to have enough space to work and carts on which to load the unwrapped pieces. It is helpful to have containers to hold packing material for reuse and recycling. As staff members unpack and unwrap, it is useful to sort the material into the necessary categories for processing, such as incoming borrowing requests (items coming from a lending library to fill a borrowing request) and lending returns (your own materials being returned from a borrowing library). You may also have items coming for different request systems, such as books from a consortial circulation system that are not processed in the same way as items coming to fill requests placed on WCRS, DOCLINE, or another system. If the area where material is unpacked also has incoming lending returns, designating the different categories of material becomes crucial.

Many large receiving operations do not unpack packages. If this is the case, those working in receiving need to understand the impact of any misdirected, lost, or damaged items. Items may arrive with or without paperwork, and the information on the request paperwork can be critical in your ability to quickly process the material and put it in the hands of the requesting patron. Therefore, it is important not to accidentally discard the paperwork with the packing materials. If an item arrives without paperwork, making a note of the sending library may be helpful in determining the status of that item. Items may also be misdirected, so it is important to train mail handlers to determine the lending or borrowing library so that you can reroute the materials as needed.

### Returnables

After the materials have been unpacked and sorted, they must be processed by library staff. Books and periodical volumes that have been sent by the lending library should be reviewed to ensure the item in hand matches the request. It is possible that a lending library will send the wrong edition or an incorrect title or will send an item to the wrong borrowing library. These materials need to be treated as problems for later handling and identification. Occasionally an item arrives that has special conditions attached. It will most likely need to be treated separately as well.

Once the item is verified against the request and the record is updated in both a local request management system and utility (e.g., DOCLINE or WCRS), staff members physically process the item by placing a wrap (bookmark or streamer) on the piece that indicates the requestor's name and the due date. This wrap is also a convenient place to reiterate policies and state return procedures. An alternative to a wrap is a bookmark. The problem with this option is that, in using the book, the patron might lose the bookmark.

It may be necessary to retain the request document that accompanies the piece in order to correctly and efficiently return the item to the lending library. If you are using a management system (e.g., Clio, ILLiad) or an ILL utility (DOCLINE, WCRS), you can choose to generate identifying paperwork at the time you return the item. A book streamer wrap allows the library to retain that paperwork without creating a separate paper file because staff can use the lending library's paperwork to help bind the strap around the book. Otherwise, you must keep the request paperwork separate from the piece while it is being used by the patron and reunite them later when the item is returned. The maintenance of such a file can be labor intensive and not necessarily the best use of limited staff time.

Some libraries also use removable labels in lieu of book straps or streamers. This should not be done if the lending library specifies that the piece should not have adhesive labels affixed to it. The Interlibrary Loan Code for the United States Explanatory Supplement states, "In particular, adhesive labels or tape should not be affixed directly to any borrowed item."[6] The Explanatory Supplement explains the rationale regarding the treatment of borrowed materials. An error in the type of label could result in permanent damage to the item and a replacement charge from the lending library. Again, it is best to be careful about using labels around these materials. Inadvertently placing a permanent label on an item may mean that staff must take time to remove it before returning the item to the lender. An alternative to placing labels on books borrowed from other libraries is to wrap scrap paper around the book and use the label to bind the paper. This allows use of the label while protecting the lending library's book.

Requesting media is a more recent development in interlibrary loan and presents a new challenge. The plastic cases holding DVDs and CDs can be fragile, and delivery of these items can be problematic for proper labeling and care. Many libraries that do loan media circulate these formats to their own patrons for short loan periods, so lending an item to another library may mean a due date different from one for print material. This information should be noted on the wrap or label so that the patron is aware and returns the material on time.

Once an item is received, identified, and wrapped or labeled, it is ready for the patron. Libraries handle patron pickup in many ways. Some libraries place the material in the ILL unit while others use the circulation desk as the primary location for pickup. Many libraries deliver directly to homes and offices. Each library must determine what is best for its operation, its patrons, and its budget. After the material is ready, the next step is to notify the patron. It is generally a good idea to make the materials available before patron notification so that a patron does not arrive at the pickup location before the materials are actually ready.

Patrons will need to be notified that the item arrived, and they should know the location and time frame for picking up the item. Some libraries leave items on the hold shelf until the due date, while others set a finite period (e.g., two weeks from date of notification) before sending unclaimed items back to the lending library. Notification can be done by e-mail, mail, or telephone. Printed notices take time and cost money to send but may be necessary in rare circumstances. Telephone calls take staff time but can be a good way to quickly notify the patron who does not have access to a computer. However, the quickest, most economical, and most widely used method is to send an e-mail. It may also be possible to send notification text messages via e-mail to a patron's cell phone. Most cell phone providers allow you to send an e-mail to a cell phone as a text message; however, character limits apply, and the user may incur charges.

### Nonreturnables

Studies have shown that the time spent in transit accounts for the majority of the total turnaround time for interlibrary loan requests.[7] Therefore, adopting a method of receiving article requests through electronic means is desired in the interest of speeding the turnaround time. As discussed in detail in chapter 6, "Technology and Web 2.0," commercial and free software is available that allows items to be scanned and sent to a requesting library electronically. Depending on the computer facilities available, it may be desirable to dedicate one workstation to receiving or sending articles electronically.

If a library uses an interlibrary loan management system (IMS), the system may automatically handle the posting of the copy to a web server as the requests arrive, notifying the patron and updating any utility without staff intervention. If you do not have software with this feature, library staff will need to process the requests for printing or posting to the Web, notify patrons, and update the request as "received" or "complete" on any utilities.

Many lending libraries supply scanned copies through e-mail. This method may be somewhat problematic depending on the size or type of file, or both, and the size of the electronic mailbox. If the item is sent in a particular format through e-mail, then the receiving library needs to determine how best to provide this document to its patron. If the receiving library has a request management system or other software for receiving electronic documents and posting to the Web, it may be able to transfer the file to these systems for receiving and delivery. A library may also choose to forward the e-mail with the attached document to the patron and update its records externally. Again, the library can experience issues with file size and mailbox size. Finally, the item can be printed and mailed to the patron.

Problems with records, such as missing pages or obscured images, may stop the posting of the piece and will need to be addressed. Some libraries review each scanned image for potential viewing issues such as black edges, blurred or unreadable print, or missing pages. Other libraries choose to post the material and wait for the patron to contact them about any problems with the quality of the copy. The thought behind posting an article without checking for completeness or quality is that by doing so, libraries are placing an emphasis on speed rather than quality. Patrons may not view all their requested documents, or they may view only a small portion rather than the entire article. Most articles are sent without quality problems, so to proof each item may be an unnecessary use of staff time and delay delivery to the patron.[8]

### ILL STATUS UPDATES

Most requests are placed via a request utility (e.g., WCRS, DOCLINE), so the next step after delivering to the patron is to update the status of the request to "received" or "complete" as required on that system. If you have a request management system, then the updating on the utility may take place automatically. If not, the staff will need to change the status in the local request system and make the appropriate updates in the external utility used for requesting the item. Updating in the local system will ensure that the patron and staff members are aware of the status of the request.

### RENEWALS, RECALLS, AND RETURNS

Interlibrary loan offices that allow renewals for borrowed material must follow the directions of the lending library. If that library does not allow renewals, then the patron should be aware of this restriction upon receiving the material. When renewals are allowed, it is best practice for the borrowing library to contact the lender in a timely way to request the renewal. A renewal request that is not acted upon by the lending library means that the borrower can assume an automatic renewal of the item.

Items may be recalled by the lending library because they are needed at the home institution. Libraries should respond immediately when receiving a recall notice. Material should be returned quickly so that the other library's patron is not inconvenienced and the relationship between the libraries endangered. If the material is still needed by the borrowing patron, then a new request should be placed with another lending library.

Once the patron has finished using the loaned material, it needs to be promptly returned to the lending library. This requires staff to update any local system or utility or both to a "returned" status. It is important to note the condition of the piece so that any damage can be covered according to the library's policy. Library staff will need to discuss the damage with the patron and contact the lending library to determine replacement or billing options. If possible, the damage to the item should be noted in the record so that follow-ups can occur. Further information about handling damaged materials can be found in the following section.

When the condition of the book is verified, the material is ready to be returned. Libraries may include return labels for their material. If it is possible, these should be retained when the material is received to make the return process easier. Packaging for special items may have been retained to help with the return. Special care should be taken with these items to ensure the material is well protected for return delivery. The library can make use of the Library Mail category provided by the United States Postal Service (USPS). The USPS also has other expedient services that assist with special handling or faster delivery. The library can also ship via a commercial courier such as UPS or FedEx or a local delivery system per the instructions of those services. If your library uses a commercial courier to track the material, it can be useful to note the tracking number on the record of the item in your local system or retain log sheets from the carrier. This information is helpful in problem solving and having it appear on the record saves time. For libraries that use manual systems it may be important to note this number in association with any other information that the library retains about the request.

## OVERDUE FEES, DAMAGED MATERIALS, AND REPLACEMENTS

Although most patrons who borrow materials respect and follow the rules and policies for borrowing, there will inevitably be items that are returned past the due date. Each borrowing library must formulate its position on overdue materials and decide whether a late fee should be charged to patrons for overdue interlibrary loan items. Some libraries take the position that fees are difficult to collect and manage. Other libraries find that having an overdue fee cuts down on those patrons who are lackadaisical about returning material in a timely manner. Another approach is to avoid overdue fines and to block the borrowing library's patron after the material has become overdue. Whatever the position of the borrowing library in relation to its users, the policy should be clearly stated both at the time the request is submitted and when the material is checked out to the patron.

It is also inevitable that borrowed materials will be damaged, lost, or stolen when in possession of the patron. The Interlibrary Loan Code of the United States puts the burden on the library that borrowed the materials to pay for loss or damages. However, a library may choose to pass these costs on to the requesting patron. The library policy on the replacement charges for this type of situation also needs to be available to the patron. If there are problems with a number of borrowing transactions, the library may need to reevaluate the patron's status as a person in "good standing" and block interlibrary loan service. There is also a chance that the lending library will determine that your library is too careless with its materials and may refuse to provide future service. This situation affects the entire borrowing institution.

If a fee will be charged for damaged, lost, or stolen material, the patron must be notified and the charges should be clearly understood. It may be possible for the borrowing library to negotiate with the lending library regarding a possible replacement copy. It is often possible to find an exact copy that can be supplied as a replacement. If the patron or the library receives permission to send a replacement copy, clarify what book condition and whether a used copy would be acceptable. Whether a library will replace an item or pay a replacement fee, action must be taken as soon as possible. Outstanding issues create more work for staff and place the association between the two libraries in peril.

## BILLING

Libraries that charge their patrons fees must have a procedure in place that is easily managed and conforms to the auditing requirements of the home institution or agency. Most libraries that collect fees have an automated management system. Some libraries accept credit cards to make the payment easier for the patron. If desired, royalty or copyright fees should be handled in the same way. Libraries should retain records pertaining to these activities as determined by their organization.

Payment of borrowing fees to the lending library should be made immediately. See "Fee Management Systems" in chapter 6 for additional information. Essentially, electronic means of exchanging funds simplifies the exchange of material without incurring the labor of invoicing payments, speeds up the reimbursement process, and maintains appropriate records regarding use for audit purposes.

International libraries may accept the International Federation of Library Associations and Institutions (IFLA) vouchers for the use of their material. Again, this system removes the billing component and exchange of money from the interaction. Libraries using this method of payment will alert the borrowing library to the number of vouchers needed for the transaction. Each voucher has a face value so it is easy for the lending library to determine how many vouchers are needed. Payment of the voucher may take place before the item is sent or following receipt.[9]

In addition to these systems, many libraries choose to use a credit card to make their payments to eliminate a delay in fulfillment or delivery. The auditing rules of a particular institution may, however, prohibit the use of these systems or a credit card, so libraries may have to rely on the traditional payment of invoices to complete the transactions. These accounts need to be kept for tracking and auditing purposes.

## CONCLUSION

Obtaining the materials needed by the patrons of the library is a challenging yet rewarding endeavor. Successful ILL operations fill a high percentage of the requests placed by patrons, deliver with a quick turnaround time, and return materials to borrowing libraries promptly. These units interact with their patrons when necessary and form relationships with other libraries to the mutual satisfaction of both institutions. Finally, libraries that continuously monitor technological advances and developments in the field will continue to provide stellar service to the library's patrons and to the institution.

## APPENDIX 2.1

### *ALA Interlibrary Loan Request Form 2002*

Request date ____________________
Need before ____________________
Request number ____________________
Client information ____________________

**Borrowing Library Name and Address**

____________________
____________________

**Citation Information**

Book author ____________________
Book title ____________________
Publisher __________ Place __________ Date __________
Series ____________________
This edition only __________ ISBN __________

Serial title ____________________
Volume/issue __________ Date __________ Pages __________
Author of article ____________________
Title of article ____________________
ISSN ____________________

Audiovisual title ____________________
Date of publication ____________________

Verified in and/or cited in ____________________
Other bibliographic number ____________________

**Lending Library Name and Address**

____________________
____________________

Lending library phone ____________________
Lending library fax ____________________
Lending library e-mail ____________________
Lending library electronic delivery address ____________________

Notes ____________________
____________________

Request complies with

- ❑ 108(g)(2) Guidelines (CCG)
- ❑ other provision of copyright law (CCL)

Authorization ____________________
Phone ____________________
Fax ____________________
E-mail ____________________
Electronic delivery address ____________________

**Type of Request**

- ❑ Loan
- ❑ Photocopy
- ❑ Estimate
- ❑ Locations

**Charge Information**

Account number ____________________

Maximum willing to pay ____________________

Have reciprocal agreement ____________________

Payment provided ____________________

**Lending Library Report**

Date of response ____________________

Date shipped ____________________

Shipped via ____________________

Insured for ____________________

Return insured ____________________

Packing requirements ____________________

Charge ____________________

Date due ____________________

**Use Restrictions**

- ❑ Library use only
- ❑ No renewals
- ❑ Copying not permitted
- ❑ Other: ____________________

**Not Sent Because**

- ❑ At bindery
- ❑ Charge exceeds limit
- ❑ Hold placed
- ❑ In process
- ❑ In use
- ❑ Lacking
- ❑ Lacks copyright compliance
- ❑ Locations not found
- ❑ Lost
- ❑ Noncirculating
- ❑ Not found as cited
- ❑ Not on shelf
- ❑ Not owned
- ❑ On order
- ❑ On reserve
- ❑ Poor condition
- ❑ Prepayment required
- ❑ Request on ____________________
- ❑ Volume/issue not yet available
- ❑ Other: ____________________

**Estimate for**

Loan ____________________

Copy ____________________

Microfilm ____________________

Microfiche ____________________

**Borrowing Library Report**

Date received ____________________

Date returned ____________________

Returned via ____________________

Insured for ____________________

Payment enclosed ❑

**Renewals**

Date requested ____________________

New due date ____________________

Renewal denied ❑

## APPENDIX 2.2

### *IFLA Interlibrary Loan Request Form*

**I.F.L.A.** INTERNATIONAL LOAN/PHOTOCOPY REQUEST FORM
FORMULAIRE DE DEMANDE DE PRET/PHOTOCOPIE INTERNATIONAL
COPY B EXEMPLAIRE B

Request ref no/Patron identifier
No de commande/identité de lecteur

Borrowing library's address
Adresse de la bibliothèque emprunteuse

Needed by
Demande avant

Quote if cost exceeds
Prix si plus que

Shelfmark
Cot de placement

Request for: ☐ Loan ☐ Photocopy ☐ Microform
Commande de: Pret Photocopie

Report/Reponse

Books: Author, title - Livres: Auteur, titre/Serials: Title, article title, author - Périodiques:Titre, titre de l'article, auteurr

Place of Publication
Lieu de publication

Publisher
Editeur

| Year-Annee | Volume-Tome | Part-No | Pages | ISBN/ISSN |
|---|---|---|---|---|
| | | | | |

Edition

Source of verification/reference
Référence bibliographique/Verification

Lending library's address/adresse de la bibliothèque prêteuse

☐ Part not held/Volume /fascisule non detenu
☐ Title not held /nous n'avons pas ce titre
☐ Not traced/Ne figure pas dans cette bibl.
☐ Not for loan/Exclu de prêt
☐ Copyright restrictions
☐ Not immediately available. Reapply in.......weeks
Non disponible actuellement. Renouvelez la demande dans.............semaines
☐ Lent until/Prêté jusqu'au......................
☐ Use in library only/A consulter sur place uniquement

I declare that this publication is required only for the purpose of research or private study.
Je déclare que cette publication n'est demandé qu'à des fins de recherche ou d'étude privée

Signature................................................

Date...............

## NOTES


1. Elaine Sanchez, ed., *Higher Education Interlibrary Loan Management Benchmarks*, 2009–2010 ed. (New York: Primary Research Group, 2009), 30.
2. Virginia Boucher, *Interlibrary Loan Practices Handbook*, 2nd ed. (Chicago: American Library Association, 1997), 4.
3. American Library Association, Interlibrary Loan Committee, Reference and User Services Association (RUSA), Interlibrary Loan Code for the United States, Interlibrary Loan Form (1994, revised 2001, revised 2008, by the Sharing and Transforming Access to Resources Section [STARS], http://www.ala.org/ala/mgrps/divs/rusa/resources/guidelines/interlibrary.cfm.
4. Lee Andrew Hilyer, "Interlibrary Loan and Document Delivery: Best Practices for Operating and Managing Interlibrary Loan Services in All Libraries; Borrowing," *Journal of Interlibrary Loan, Document Delivery and Electronic Reserve* 16, no. 1–2 (2006): 28.
5. Libraries Very Interested in Sharing (LVIS), http://www.cyberdriveillinois.com/departments/library/who_we_are/OCLC/lvis.html.
6. American Library Association, Interlibrary Loan Committee, Reference and User Services Association (RUSA), Interlibrary Loan Code for the United States Explanatory Supplement, 4.8, http://www.ala.org/ala/mgrps/divs/rusa/resources/guidelines/interlibrary.cfm.
7. Mary E. Jackson, *Measuring the Performance of Interlibrary Loan Operations in North American Research and College Libraries* (Washington, DC: Association of Research Libraries, 1998).

8. Ruth S. Connell and Karen L. Janke, "Turnaround Time between ILLiad's Odyssey and Ariel Delivery Methods: A Comparison," *Journal of Interlibrary Loan, Document Delivery and Electronic Reserve* 16, no. 3 (2006): 41–56.
9. Christine Robben and Cherié L. Weible, "International Payment: Methods to Consider," *Journal of Interlibrary Loan, Document Delivery and Information Supply* 12, no. 3 (2002): 29–35.

## BIBLIOGRAPHY

Boucher, Virginia. *Interlibrary Loan Practices Handbook.* 2nd ed. Chicago: American Library Association, 1997.

Connell, Ruth S., and Karen L. Janke. "Turnaround Time between ILLiad's Odyssey and Ariel Delivery Methods: A Comparison." *Journal of Interlibrary Loan, Document Delivery and Electronic Reserve* 16, no. 3 (2006): 41–56.

Hilyer, Lee Andrew. "Interlibrary Loan and Document Delivery: Best Practices for Operating and Managing Interlibrary Loan Services in All Libraries; Borrowing." *Journal of Interlibrary Loan, Document Delivery and Electronic Reserve* 16, no. 1–2 (2006): 17–39.

Hoffert, Barbara. "It's the Economy." *Library Journal* 134, no. 3 (2009): 34–36.

Jackson, Mary E. *Assessing ILL/DD Services: New Cost-Effective Alternatives.* Washington, DC: Association of Research Libraries, 2004.

———. "Assessing ILL/DD Services Study: Initial Observations." *ARL: A Bimonthly Report on Issues and Actions,* no. 230/231 (2003): 21–22.

———. "Forms, Forms, Forms." *Wilson Library Bulletin* 69 (1995): 70–71+.

———. "The Ideal ILL Service Model." *Wilson Library Bulletin* 60 (1995): 68–69+.

———. "Library to Library: ILL; Issues and Actions." *Wilson Library Bulletin* 65 (1991): 102–105.

———. "Looking Back and Looking Ahead: The Best Is Yet to Come." *American Libraries* 31, no. 10 (2000): 47.

———. "Measuring Performance, Applying Results, Improving Service." *InCite* (Australian Library and Information Association) 22 (2001).

———. *Measuring the Performance of Interlibrary Loan Operations in North American Research and College Libraries.* Washington, DC: Association of Research Libraries, 1998.

Kelsey, Paul, ed. *Profiles of Best Practices in Academic Library Interlibrary Loan.* New York: Primary Research Group, 2009.

Kohn, Karen. "Finding It Free." *Journal of Interlibrary Loan, Document Delivery and Electronic Reserve* 16, no. 3 (2006): 57–65.

Leon, Lars E., June L. DeWeese, Carol Ann Kochan, Billie Peterson-Lugo, and Brian L. Pytlik Zillig. "Enhanced Resource Sharing through Group Interlibrary Loan Best Practices: A Conceptual, Structural, and Procedural Approach." *Libraries and the Academy* 3, no. 3 (2003): 419–30.

Leykam, Andrew. "Exploring Interlibrary Loan Usage Patterns and Liaison Activities: The Experience at a U.S. University." *Interlending and Document Supply* 36, no. 4 (2008): 218–24.

Line, Maurice B., Elda-Monica Guerrero, Mary E. Jackson, Niels Mark, Henri Sene, and Leo Waaijers. "The Future of Interlibrary Loan and Document Supply: Views and Comments." *Interlending and Document Supply* 30, no. 2 (2002): 60–65.

Luo, Lili, David West, and Gary Marchionini. "Annotations of Interlibrary Loan Process." *Journal of Interlibrary Loan, Document Delivery and Electronic Reserve* 18, no. 3 (2008): 307–24.

Meyers, Pat L., Wilbur A. Stolt, and Yem S. Fong, eds. *Interlibrary Loan/Document Delivery and Customer Satisfaction: Strategies for Redesigning Services*. New York: Haworth Press, 2006.

Poe, Jodi. "Common Practices in Interlibrary Loan, Document Delivery and Electronic Reserves." *Journal of Interlibrary Loan, Document Delivery and Electronic Reserve* 18, no. 2 (2008): 125–28.

Posner, Beth. "Library Resource Sharing in the Early Age of Google." *Library Philosophy and Practice* 9, no. 3 (Summer 2007): 1–10.

Reighart, Renee, and Cyril Oberlander. "Exploring the Future of Interlibrary Loan; Generalizing the Experience of the University of Virginia, USA." *Interlending and Document Supply* 36, no. 4 (2008): 184–90.

Robben, Christine, and Cherié L. Weible. "International Payment: Methods to Consider." *Journal of Interlibrary Loan, Document Delivery and Information Supply* 12, no. 3 (2002): 29–35.

Sanchez, Elaine, ed. *Higher Education Interlibrary Loan Management Benchmarks*. 2009–2010 ed. New York: Primary Research Group, 2009.

Smith, Michelle. "Two Major Strategies for Facilitating Increased Interlibrary Loan Patron Satisfaction." *Georgia Library Quarterly* 45, no. 2 (2008): 9–11.

Stein, Joan. "IFLA Guidelines for Best Practice for Interlibrary Loan and Document Delivery." *Journal of Access Service* 5, no. 1 (2007): 295–303.

Zheng Ye Yang. "The Ten Commandments of Interlibrary Loan Borrowing, Interlibrary Loan Lending, and Shipping and General Conduct." *Journal of Interlibrary Loan, Document Delivery and Electronic Reserve* 19, no. 1 (2009): 95–100.

CHAPTER THREE

# LENDING WORKFLOW BASICS

*Amy R. Paulus*

INTERLIBRARY LOAN consists of a relationship between two libraries: the borrower and the lender. Great responsibilities are attached to providing the service of loaning local materials to other libraries. Policies and procedures for lending will be covered in this chapter. Libraries of all sizes and types that lend their materials to other libraries will find helpful information here, regardless of the amount of requests processed, the number of staff available, or the length of time an interlibrary loan service has been provided.

## POLICIES

Having policies in place to govern the lending of materials from your library will help to prevent a delay in service and to avoid a potential disagreement with another library.

### Informing Potential Borrowers

All lending libraries should have a statement that details the service they will provide. There are a variety of ways to inform potential borrowers about who will be lent to, what will or will not be lent, in what time frame, by what method, and for what cost. One convenient way for the lending library to provide this information is to maintain a web page devoted to interlibrary lending. This web page should, at a minimum, contain contact information (e-mail, phone, mailing address, fax), charges and billing information, collections that are not eligible for interlibrary loan, a link or URL to the online catalog, and information about the electronic delivery of scanned or photocopied material such as an Ariel or Odyssey address (Ariel and Odyssey are two types of software used for electronic transmission; see chapter 6, "Technology and Web 2.0," for further information) or about loan delivery methods (e.g., United States Postal Service, UPS, FedEx, DHL). It is also helpful to include information about hours of operation or closure days, loan period and renewal policy, photocopy policy, rush service, affiliations, federal tax ID number (FEIN), and relevant lending symbols associated with the library. Chapter 5, "Management of Interlibrary Loan," includes a more detailed discussion of policy development.

Lending libraries can also share policy information within interlibrary loan systems. For example, OCLC has a WorldCat Registry that is available for viewing by all on the Web. As a lender, creating and keeping this information current is of benefit to you and potential borrowers as it contains contact information. Any library can create an account and have a profile with the library's information. OCLC's Policies Directory is tied directly to an OCLC authorization but contains much more detail than the WorldCat Registry. If you lend via OCLC, contact information, policies, charges, and other information about your services should be entered and maintained here.

### Limiting Borrowing Libraries

In an ideal word, all interlibrary loan requests would be filled by lending libraries. However, there are many logical and logistical reasons why this does not happen. Your lending policy should specify what types of libraries you will not lend to. International locations, for example, can be logistically and cost prohibitive. In addition, individuals are traditionally not lent to directly but are instead referred to their closest affiliated library. For students, this is often their academic institution's library, which can be a large university or a small rural high school. For the public, ILL services usually come from a local or regional library. Sometimes libraries only lend to a specific group or within a consortium. If there are any restrictions on borrowers, your policy statement must clearly identify these to prevent a borrowing library from submitting a request that will not be honored.

### Specifying Request Methods

Borrowing libraries should have a variety of ways to submit a request. These options should be articulated in your policies. If there are ways a request is not accepted, these should also be noted. If your ILL management system provides an online method by which a borrower can submit a request directly, include instructions for this process in your policy statement.

### Choosing Materials to Lend

Libraries often have collections that are unique or have formats that, for a variety of reasons, cannot be lent on interlibrary loan. For example, media collections, especially in more fragile formats such as vinyl records, or special collections—especially rare or expensive items—may be restricted from the interlibrary loan service. These formats or collections should be clearly stated in your policies so that potential borrowers know ahead of time not to request something from that particular area. Sometimes there are items, often in special collections or archives, for which the department must be contacted directly. Any groups of items that are not lent collectively must be clearly listed in the policies.

OCLC WorldCat Resource Sharing allows you to set up deflections so that a submitted request that fits the defined criteria will automatically move on to the next lender or be sent back unfilled to the borrower. The lending library will not even see this request, except in monthly reports. Deflections can be set up to block requests based on format, OCLC group, borrower maximum cost, or material age. Although the hope is that interlibrary loan lending be as liberal as possible, it is wise to make policies clear about what will not be lent and to set up deflections in OCLC judiciously.

### Establishing Turnaround Time and Loan Periods

Staffing, equipment, and delivery systems all affect the time required to process and complete an interlibrary loan request. Information about the time frame for both regular and rush processing should be clearly articulated so that potential borrowers know up front when they can expect their request to be filled. Planned closures or other times when service will not be available should also be listed in your policies. Busy libraries often receive many requests and may have to prioritize or deny requests based on the relationship with the requesting library. Consortial, regional, or other agreements with libraries often take precedence over libraries with which there is no documented relationship.

The loan period and renewal time should also be articulated in the policies so that borrowers know ahead of time how long their users will have the materials. Loan and renewal periods should be set to allow adequate time for shipping, use, and return delivery.

### Selecting Delivery Methods

Materials can be delivered to a borrowing library by many different methods, depending on the type of request—loan (known as a returnable) or photocopy (often referred to as a nonreturnable). Although a borrowing library should specify its preferred method of delivery (which should be honored if possible), it is best to include in your policy statement information about what types of delivery you can provide. For returnables, UPS, FedEx, or the United States Postal Service are examples of ways to ship materials to the borrowing library. For nonreturnables, Ariel, Odyssey, fax, PDF via e-mail, PDF via posting on website, or the United States Postal Service are examples of ways to deliver photocopied or scanned materials. Any and all methods that a lending library uses to provide materials should be clearly stated in the policies.

### Setting Fees

For a variety of reasons and circumstances, borrowing libraries might be unable to pay a fee for interlibrary loan services. It is crucial to include information about any charges associated with an interlibrary loan transaction. Many libraries are involved in consortial or reciprocal agreements that allow each library to borrow freely from the others. For libraries not participating in or eligible for such an arrangement, your policy should clearly state how much you charge for each request and whether this fee differs for returnables and nonreturnables. Rush, fax, or extra services, if available, should also be defined if charges are associated with them. Information about how payment is accepted should also be included. Not all libraries are equipped to handle some methods of payment, such as credit cards, and the borrowing library should see this information in the policies.

## PROCEDURES

Once policies have been defined and are available to borrowing libraries, the next step is to begin receiving and filling requests. There are many ways to manage this workflow, and each library will have unique circumstances, especially in terms of volume, staffing, equipment, support, and supplies. Generally, all libraries should consider the following guidelines.

### Accepting and Processing Requests

Lending libraries can receive requests by several different means. Regardless of the method you use to receive requests, it is essential that they be checked and processed at least daily and more frequently if possible. Requests can be submitted by fax, e-mail, online request form, mail, OCLC WorldCat Resource Sharing, Ariel, Rapid, DOCLINE, a local ILL management system, or an ILS (integrated library system). If your library uses an ILL management system to manage requests, the company that owns or manages the software has put workflows and procedures in place. Appropriate training from this company is essential in order to fully use all features and to process requests correctly and efficiently. Whether the request is being processed electronically within a management system or manually with another method, several criteria should be examined before processing proceeds: the maxcost (the maximum amount a borrower is willing to pay); the date needed by; the requested method of delivery (such as fax for a nonreturnable or UPS for a returnable); any special instructions; and the appropriate copyright statement (if a nonreturnable). If any of these criteria cannot be met or are in violation of your policies, the request must be answered that same day citing the reason for nonfulfillment. An ILL management system can do this immediately. For requests received outside a management system, the borrowing library should be notified by whatever method it has indicated.

### Verifying Requests with the Local Catalog

After the initial screening is done, the next step is to verify that the material requested is owned by the library and that it is available. Familiarity with the local OPAC, card catalog, or other finding aids for library materials is essential for this phase. Instruction on searching, if not already included in a training plan, should be provided. There are many intricacies to library catalogs, particularly in serial records, and careful attention must be paid in order to correctly identify what is owned. If the item requested is not available, the reason should be communicated to the borrowing library. OCLC WorldCat Resource Sharing and other software systems that communicate directly with each other have a standard set of reasons. OCLC's standardized language for its cancellations is shown in figure 3.1.

The reason selected for cancellation should be as accurate as possible. The more specific a reason the better, as this will help the borrower decide whether to try a different lender or resubmit the request with more information. If the request was submitted via a paper-based method, the borrower should be notified by this same method or by whichever method the borrower has requested. However the request is answered, it should be done promptly and with as much information as necessary to help the borrowing library.

Because lending interlibrary loan staff members spend a significant amount of time searching the online catalog, any errors in the records of the physical volume should be dealt with immediately. Common errors that you may find include broken links to e-journals, inaccurate serial holdings, items that are missing or no longer held, and incorrectly cataloged items. Reporting these errors will help the next user find the information more quickly. If OCLC is used for cataloging and interlibrary loan, it is important to report discrepancies between the local catalog

**Figure 3.1** Reasons for No (in order by frequency of use)

1. In Use/On Loan
2. Noncirculating
3. Not on Shelf/Missing
4. Not Owned
5. Lacking Volume/Issue
6. Branch Policy Problem
7. On Order
8. Cost Exceeds Limit
9. Technical Processing
10. Preferred Delivery Time Not Possible
11. Poor Condition
12. At Bindery
13. Volume Issue Not Yet Available
14. Not Licensed to Fill
15. Required Delivery Services Not Supported
16. Prepayment Required
17. Other

Source: http://lists.webjunction.org/wjlists/ill-l/2008-July/024127.html

and OCLC. If you have canceled a request because you do not own the item but OCLC WorldCat reflects ownership, the item should be reported to the appropriate library staff so that OCLC can be updated. This correction will prevent other libraries from requesting the same material from you in the future. Also, if your library subscribes to a variety of electronic journals and a particular link is not working, report this problem to library staff to prevent future users from encountering the same problem.

### Verifying Licensing Terms for Electronic Materials

Electronic serials and books are ubiquitous in libraries in the twenty-first century, and verifying availability for these materials includes consulting the licensing agreement associated with the item. Licensing terms vary between libraries. Some content is strictly unavailable for ILL purposes, other content can be used but only if certain conditions are met, and still other content is available without restriction for the purpose of ILL. If the license terms do not allow ILL, report this restriction to the borrowing library. OCLC WorldCat Resource Sharing has a "Not Licensed to Fill" category that was recently created for this very purpose. Some libraries have an electronic resources management software system that records and communicates specific licensing terms to library staff. ILL personnel should have access to this system or at least to the licensing information related to ILL. If an electronic resources management system is not available or used, it is important to find the interlibrary loan terms on a license and record this information in the ILL department. The terms of the license should be upheld. Regular communication with library staff who are responsible for licensing will ensure that ILL staff are aware of any new or updated license information.

### Retrieving the Item

If the print item is owned and available, the call number or other location-specific information should be noted on the request. Borrowers might request a particular edition or year, so careful attention should be paid to make sure the call number and item are an exact match. All requests should be collected and sorted by location and the items pulled from the stacks at least daily. Sometimes materials cannot be located on the shelf. If you are the last library available to fill the request and have staff available to do so, items not located on the shelf after an initial search should be re-verified and re-searched. If an item is not found after a second search, the borrower should be notified immediately by canceling the request. To ensure accuracy for your own users, report items not found to the appropriate department so they can be officially declared missing and replaced.

Problems also arise with the citations of requests, particularly for journal articles. If an article cannot be located or if the bibliographic information specified on the request is incorrect, a lender should take some time to verify the citation. If the citation is still problematic, report the situation to the borrower. If the correct citation is found but the item is not owned by the lender, the borrower should be informed. Staffing and time constraints often make it difficult to do such follow-up, but it is a service that should be provided if possible.

All requests for items that need to be pulled from the stacks should be gathered and sorted by location. For example, if your library has multiple levels, the requests should be sorted by floor. In a smaller library, requests might be sorted by fiction and nonfiction so retrieval is more efficient. Physically retrieving these items is the next step.

Retrieved items, along with their request forms, should be sorted. A first sort might be to separate the returnables (loans) from the nonreturnables (i.e., scans or photocopies). Consortial or other agreements might give a certain category of borrowers a higher priority, so these requests, rush requests, or others needing priority should be sorted out and placed in a specified area for processing first.

### Processing Returnables (Loans)

The processing of nonreturnables and returnables is quite different. Returnables must be checked out in the ILS (local circulation system) and the ILL management system, if available, to accurately track and communicate their status. Procedures for checking out materials in the ILS vary. Some libraries assign each borrowing library its own circulation record, while others collectively check out all ILL materials to one ILL account. However checkout is done, keeping these records up to date is essential so that local users are aware that the material is not available and the ILL department can manage and track these requests easily. If a separate ILL management system is used, materials must be updated there as well. With some systems, such as ILLiad, this updating will trigger the appropriate action within OCLC WorldCat Resource Sharing so that the request is at the appropriate status. For all these systems, it is best to provide a loan period that accurately reflects the time the materials will be out of the building. If the material is lent for four weeks to the borrower, shipping time to and from the borrowing library must also be taken into account; thus, a total loan period of six weeks would be adequate. It is best to be as generous as possible, without hindering access for local users. The option for renewal should be available for all materials, and a period of at least four weeks is standard. However, there may be circumstances that will create exceptions to a standard loan period.

In addition to exceptions for a standard loan period for ILL materials, some materials may require special handling or conditions for lending. It is best to obtain the borrowing library's acceptance of these requirements before the item is lent. Some materials, special collections items in particular, often are restricted to use within the borrower's library, must be returned via a traceable method, or have a high replacement cost value. Because not all borrowing libraries have the appropriate facilities or budgets to accept such conditions, it is a courtesy to communicate any requirement well ahead of time to allow the borrower to refuse the loan. If the borrower accepts the conditions, they should be stated clearly on the paperwork or book strap and be attached to or included with the book.

Once an item is retrieved from the shelves, it must be prepared for shipment to the borrowing library. Paperwork or labeling should accompany the material that shows when and to where the material must be returned, who the material is going to, how many pieces are being sent, and any special instructions. Some ILL management systems can produce request-specific book straps or labels that can be attached directly to the item. Book straps are strips of paper that are attached around the front cover of the book although nothing is taped or secured directly to the book. This method is highly recommended to reduce loss of paperwork and to prevent potential damage from sticky label or tape residue. If an ILL management system is not used, printouts or photocopies of the request should be included in the front pages of the book so that the borrower has the appropriate information about the loan.

In addition to the paperwork about the loan, two shipping labels must be prepared: one with the correct address for the borrowing library and one with a return address that the borrowing library can use. When using companies such as UPS or FedEx, use a street address in lieu of a P.O. box or generic address to prevent extra charges or delay in delivery. Note also that some large libraries have separate addresses for their borrowing and lending activities or for different branches or subject libraries.

Packaging materials are also needed to send the items safely and accurately. Boxes or padded envelopes are highly recommended to protect items during the journey from one library to the other. This protection is especially important for formats other than printed books, such as DVDs, vinyl records, VHS tapes, or other audiovisual materials. Avoid using padded envelopes containing paper fiber padding as they can be torn by sharp corners. Packaging and processing of the materials may take place outside the ILL department, such as in a library's centralized shipping or mail room. Regardless of where shipping occurs, it is best practice to send the item as quickly as possible so the borrower receives the item as quickly as possible.

Special insurance for an item's replacement value may be necessary, especially if an item is expensive, unique, or fragile.

Shipping to international locations often requires additional steps. The appropriate customs form must be filled out accurately and included with the item. If the lender does not have these forms or is sending items internationally for the first time, more information about this process can be obtained by contacting the United States Postal Service, either online or at a local post office. It is also important to be aware of the variety of ways to ship materials and the consequences of using each method. For example, shipping materials via a shipping company often results in long delays or holds at customs. For overseas locations, shipping by airmail is usually the fastest method although it does have additional costs. Whatever means of shipping you select, pay special attention to any delivery method requests from the borrower as this may prevent delays or customs duties.

Before materials leave the lending library, a final check should be performed to make sure that the correct item is being sent to the correct shipping address. It is also important to make sure that the material itself is appropriately marked with ownership stamps or library markings, especially in the case of microfiche or microfilm. These materials often are not marked directly, so the boxes or sleeves must have the appropriate ownership marks. Additionally, if materials have security strips in them to trigger an alarm system, they should be desensitized so that they will not set off alarms or cause other disruptions at the borrowing library. The condition of the book should also be noted before shipping. A book in poor condition may be further damaged during shipping and use by the borrower. It is best, therefore, not to send such materials and instead route them to the conservation department or other repair personnel.

### Processing Nonreturnables (Scans or Photocopies)

As with returnables, fulfilling requests for nonreturnables requires certain supplies and equipment. With electronic delivery highly desirable and prevalent, owning or having access to a good scanner should be a high priority. Transmissions by fax or mail have decreased but are still viable methods of delivery, and the supplies necessary to provide this service should be readily available. The requests should be sorted by method of delivery and then prioritized to make sure the oldest requests or requests with consortial obligations for delivery time are processed first.

Depending on the delivery method and available equipment, workflows will differ among libraries. Requests for which the borrower has specified postal mail delivery will need to be photocopied, stamped with the appropriate copyright information (see the accompanying box, "Warning Concerning Copyright Restrictions"), placed in an appropriately sized envelope, addressed to the correct shipping location, and placed in the mail for delivery to the borrowing library. Items needing to be faxed must be photocopied, stamped with the appropriate copyright information, and faxed to the borrower's number. Multifunctional equipment is becoming more popular, and one machine can often fax, scan, or photocopy materials via a document feeder or a flat scanning bed or both. Some machines can scan an item and send a PDF to an e-mail address as well. For other requests requiring electronic delivery, the process will again depend on the available equipment and software. Ariel software can scan and send items electronically to another Ariel library based on IP address. It also can scan and send a PDF via e-mail or post to a server. The Odyssey component in ILLiad or the free stand-alone version of Odyssey provides a method for scanned materials to be transmitted to other Odyssey/ILLiad libraries.

It is important to include a copyright statement with each article. An example of a copyright statement is shown in the accompanying box.

However the material is delivered, a clear, complete, and legible copy should be provided. Leaving adequate margins, scanning or photocopying one page per page, including illustrations or additional sections, and using advanced features on scanners such as image dithering or finger masking will ensure the best copy. Each request should be updated within the appropriate system, such as OCLC WorldCat

**Warning Concerning Copyright Restrictions**

The copyright law of the United States (Title 17, United States Code) governs the making of photocopies or other reproductions of copyrighted material. Under certain conditions specified in the law, libraries and archives are authorized to furnish a photocopy or other reproduction. One of these specific conditions is that the photocopy or reproduction is not to be "used for any purpose other than private study, scholarship, or research." If a user makes a request for, or later uses, a photocopy or reproduction for purposes in excess of "fair use," that user may be liable for copyright infringement. This institution reserves the right to refuse to accept a copying order if, in its judgment, fulfillment of the order would involve violation of copyright law.

Notice: This material may be protected by copyright law (Title 17, U.S. Code).

Resource Sharing, to reflect that the material has been shipped, either in conjunction with providing the material or very shortly afterward. Updating is essential to ensure that the status is appropriate for borrower updating to occur. In OCLC WorldCat Resource Sharing, if a request is not updated before it passes to the next lender, the borrower might receive the item and try to update the system to show receipt. This action may cause problems and could result in the request moving on to the next lender, which will then provide the same material to the borrower and receive the credit for doing so.

Occasionally, borrowing libraries will request photocopies to use as replacement pages for materials that have had pages torn out or otherwise mutilated. Special instructions on how the borrower would like the pages photocopied, which may not coincide with an exact article, should be followed. If the request cannot be filled as specified, it is best to consider lending the entire item so the borrower can obtain the necessary photocopy.

### Charging for Transactions

For all interlibrary loan requests that are not covered by a reciprocal agreement, the lending library must be able to issue bills and receive payment. If the transaction occurs in OCLC WorldCat Resource Sharing and the borrower has specified it accepts being billed in this manner in its maxcost field, payment can be made via the ILL Fee Management (IFM) system. The financial transaction takes place upon completion of the request in OCLC WorldCat Resource Sharing. This method of billing, especially when the borrower is a participating library of IFM, should be used as much as possible. There are several time- and cost-saving benefits for using IFM within OCLC WorldCat Resource Sharing: invoicing is a single monthly charge or is credited directly to your OCLC account; additional staff are not required to produce, manage, and follow up invoices and their payments; and lending credits are issued by OCLC that can be used toward subscription or other costs. Using IFM to handle invoicing for an international library is also seamless as the transaction does not depend on currency conversion.

If the interlibrary loan transaction takes place outside OCLC WorldCat Resource Sharing or if the borrowing library does not participate in the IFM system, invoices must be prepared. The borrower should expect such an invoice either because an appropriate amount was indicated in a maxcost field or because the lender notified the borrowing library of the charge before processing the request. Depending on workflows, software, systems, and personnel, managing the financial aspect of an interlibrary loan transaction varies widely among libraries. However this process is handled, it should be done promptly so that the borrower can verify the charges and send payment. Sending an invoice along with the material is efficient and will help the borrower match the invoice to the transaction. If the lender's ILL management system or other accounting program cumulates invoices and sends them out on a timed basis, such as once a month, it is imperative that the invoice contain enough information for the borrower to identify the request: transaction number, patron name, title, transaction date, the charge, and contact information for questions and for sending of payment.

For international lending, vouchers issued by the International Federation of Library Associations and Institutions (IFLA) are another method of receiving payment without having to worry about conversion or the correct currency. An IFLA voucher is a plastic reusable ticket that is exchanged between libraries instead of a monetary payment. The advantages are many: less staff time spent issuing and managing invoices, less time spent converting currency rates, and no bank charges for this type of transaction. These vouchers can be accumulated by the lending library and submitted for payment from IFLA headquarters, or they can be used by the borrowing department to pay for any international transactions. If the borrowing international library participates in this program, the lending library should send an invoice and indicate the number of IFLA vouchers required. The number of vouchers should correspond to normal interlibrary loan charges. If the fee is $25, for example, the invoice should ask for three vouchers to cover the cost.

Many libraries participate in some type of reciprocal agreement with another library. In some states an official statewide system allows for free interlibrary loan transactions among the member libraries, while in other states it is unwritten practice to provide free service to other libraries within the state. State libraries or state library associations are often able to explain the available options. Other libraries are members of groups based on geography or type of library. Libraries Very Interested in Sharing (LVIS) is a large OCLC group that has very general criteria for membership and allows free interlibrary loan activity among its members. An individual library can also seek a one-on-one reciprocal agreement with another library. The majority of such requests are initiated by a borrowing library and should be seriously considered and accepted when feasible. The advantage of doing so is the reduction in management of invoicing for both lending and borrowing transactions.

### Processing Returns

Once the material has left the building, the next step for returnables is normally at the end of the request's lifespan: the processing of the material when it is returned by the borrowing library. The first step is to verify that the correct item or number of pieces has been returned and that the material is in the same condition as when it left the lending library. Next, the book must be discharged in the local circulation system, sensitized (if applicable), and reshelved. If a local ILL management system is used, the request also must be updated in this system to complete the transaction. Returns should be processed as promptly as possible to ensure that the material is available for the next user and that the transaction is cleared on the borrower's end as well.

### Processing Renewals

Sometimes a borrower's user needs the materials for longer than the specified loan period. The borrower should initiate a request for a renewal several days before the due date. Information about the renewal should have been included on the paperwork or book strap that was sent with the book. If renewals are not possible, the request should be immediately denied so that the borrower can retrieve the material from the user and return it promptly. However, renewal requests should be honored, especially if the material is not needed locally. Borrowers can request renewals via several different methods. If the transaction has occurred within an ILL system such as OCLC WorldCat Resource Sharing, the renewal request should arrive through this system. For transactions that have taken place outside such a system, the borrower may e-mail, fax, or phone a renewal request. However renewal requests are received, it is important to consistently and promptly answer them. Additionally, if a local ILL management system is used, both it and the local ILS must be updated to reflect the new due date.

### Handling Overdue Materials

Unfortunately, not all interlibrary loan transactions are completed within the specified time frame. There are cases, all outside the lending library's control, in which a returnable is not returned by the due date. Handling this process promptly and with a friendly demeanor is necessary to maintain good relationships with borrowing libraries. It is often best to wait several days after the due date before sending an overdue notice to the borrowing library. This delay will allow items in transit to your library to arrive, which will save staff time for both the lending and borrowing libraries.

After a grace period of at least seven days, overdue notices should be sent to each library with an overdue item. Many local ILL management systems can send these notices, and I recommend taking advantage of this automated workflow management. Some libraries opt for overdue notices to be generated from their ILS, but it is best not to send them from more than one system. If possible, overdue notifications should be e-mailed to ensure fast delivery. However, not all libraries are equipped to handle this format and not all borrowing libraries have a readily available e-mail address. In those cases, overdue notices should be printed and sent in the mail or faxed. The frequency for sending overdue notices will depend on staffing levels but should be at least monthly. If possible and especially for those libraries that lend large quantities, weekly notices are more desirable. Fining libraries for overdue materials should be avoided as well. The staff time spent sending and collecting such fees is often not worth the cost for the small amount that is owed. To encourage the return of overdue items, libraries can be blocked from borrowing until the items are returned. This practice should be used sparingly, if at all. Additionally, if an item is overdue for an unreasonable period of time, the borrowing library can be charged for the replacement value of the item. However, regular communication with the borrowing library should take place before any of these steps are implemented.

Occasionally, a user from the lending library will need a book that has been sent out on interlibrary loan. The borrowing library should be notified immediately that the item has been recalled and should be returned as soon as possible. Notifications can happen via phone, e-mail, and fax but also must occur within any automated system. OCLC WorldCat Resource Sharing can update the record to "recalled," which also places the request in a special messages queue for the borrower. If there is a local ILL management system, the item can be recalled through this system as well. Whatever method is used, requests in recall status should continue to be monitored, and the borrowing library should receive regular updates, either by having the recalled requests fall into the regular overdue notification schedule or by having them handled separately and individually.

### Completing the Transaction

It is the responsibility of the lending library to make sure that the request has been successfully filled and completed. Problems sometimes arise in the transaction, for both returnables and nonreturnables. Problems that are discovered or reported by the borrowing library should be dealt with immediately.

Nonreturnables, whether provided as scanned documents or as photocopies, can get lost in transit. E-mail filters, Internet connections, server lapses, or human error can all cause disruption of the delivery of a scanned or photocopied item. Systems, such as OCLC WorldCat Resource Sharing, have an automated trigger if a request has not been updated to the next step within a certain time. However the discrepancy is reported, the lending library should respond immediately to a request for the item to be resupplied. If the material is delivered, it might have missing pages, have text that is cut off, have unreadable text or charts, or just be the wrong thing. The borrowing library should report such problems immediately, and the lending library should respond quickly.

Returnables face similar problems. Materials loaned can be lost in the mail, damaged during transit, or sent to the wrong library, or the wrong title can be supplied. Although careful processing of requests should eliminate most such problems, mistakes can sometimes occur. Some problems can be reported immediately, such as an item that is physically damaged or that is the wrong title. If the wrong title has been sent, the correct volume should be identified and sent to the borrower immediately. If the item is damaged and the lender has insured it, the appropriate forms should be filled out or the appropriate people contacted to obtain money to either replace or repair the item. If it was shipped without insurance, the lender has the right to ask the borrowing library to pay for the damages. Materials that do not arrive at all should be traced. The trace may verify that the item was received by the borrowing library, or it may show that the item was received at a different location. Wherever the item ended up, attempts should be made to locate it and have it delivered to the correct location. If the material is truly lost, the borrowing library is responsible for the replacement cost. Some lending libraries will allow a borrower to purchase an exact copy of the item rather than pay for a replacement. This practice would need to be mutually agreed upon and must be an acceptable alternative for the lending library's collection and processing needs. Depending on the size and staff of the lending library, any lost or replaced item needs to be reported to the appropriate circulation, acquisition, or cataloging department as well.

## STATISTICS

Interlibrary loan transactions can provide a wealth of information about your collection as well as the importance of this service. Gathering and managing statistics for lending transactions should be included in your procedures. Local ILL management systems or other automated programs often provide reports and other statistical data on a daily, monthly, and yearly basis. At a minimum, an annual report should be prepared that details the activity of interlibrary loan lending. The ability to articulate who you are lending to and in what quantities is invaluable for the justification of your services, and the library director and administration should be aware of this information. These data are particularly valuable when additional staffing or equipment is needed. If a lending library does not have access to an automated method for collecting statistics, they must be gathered manually. At a minimum, you should count how many returnables were filled, how many non-returnables were filled, and how many requests went unfilled. Interlibrary loan information also can be helpful when assessing your own collection, identifying ways to streamline procedures, and evaluating policies. Further information on statistics can be found in chapter 5, "Management of Interlibrary Loan."

## CONCLUSION

Interlibrary loan lending is important in the resource-sharing world, because if no one lent, no one could borrow. Given the realities of restrictive budgets, a library cannot purchase everything that is needed by its users, nor can it anticipate these needs. Interlibrary loan lending allows a borrowing library to expand its collection, albeit on a temporary basis, and is a service based on reciprocity. Without the generosity of a lending library, library users everywhere would not have access to collections outside their local libraries.

CHAPTER FOUR

# U.S. COPYRIGHT AND INTERLIBRARY LOAN PRACTICE

*Cindy Kristof*

INTERLIBRARY LOAN (ILL) practitioners, like others working in libraries, react to the topic of copyright in a variety of ways. Some see a mild nuisance, some a menacing specter; most see something in between. However, at least for ILL, copyright does not need to be viewed with fear. Practice in this area of librarianship is largely well established, supported by both law and agreed-upon guidelines. As Lee Andrew Hilyer writes, "An extensive knowledge of every nuance of copyright law is not required for successful (and legal) operation of an ILL department."[1]

The original purpose of copyright law, as established in 1788 by the ratified United States Constitution, was "to promote the Progress of Science and useful Arts by securing for limited Times to Authors and Inventors the exclusive Right to their respective Writings and Discoveries." This protection was meant to encourage scientific progress, innovation, and invention. The purpose of ILL as defined by the Interlibrary Loan Code for the United States is "to obtain, upon request of a library user, material not available in the user's local library."[2] ILL does not exist to contravene copyright or to undercut commercial publishers' profits; rather, ILL and copyright law are meant to work together harmoniously, in order for libraries to provide the widest possible access to copyrighted works by their patrons. This access naturally benefits society as a whole.

## LAWS AND GUIDELINES

In the United States, copyright law is federal law and is contained in Title 17 of the United States Code. Although detailed knowledge of copyright law is unnecessary, it does help ILL practitioners to have a basic foundation on which an understanding of the applicable laws and guidelines can be built. Outlined in the following paragraphs are Sections 106 through 109, the most relevant to ILL practice.

### Section 106—Exclusive Rights of Copyright Owners

As part of the 1976 Copyright Act, the copyright owner—not necessarily the author or creator—is granted the following six exclusive rights in copyrighted works:

- **to reproduce the copyrighted work in copies** or phonorecord
- **to prepare derivative works** based upon the copyrighted work
- **to distribute copies** or phonorecords of the copyrighted work to the public by sale or other transfer of ownership, or by rental, lease, or lending
- in the case of literary, musical, dramatic, and choreographic works, pantomimes, and motion pictures and other audiovisual works, **to perform the copyrighted work publicly**
- in the case of literary, musical, dramatic, and choreographic works, pantomimes, and pictorial, graphic, or sculptural works, including the individual images of a motion picture or other audiovisual work, **to display the copyrighted work publicly**
- in the case of sound recordings, **to perform the copyrighted work publicly** by means of a digital audio transmission

Note that the reproduction and distribution of copies of a work are exclusive rights; however, reproduction and distribution are precisely what ILL departments need to do. Therefore, there are exceptions to Section 106 in the law. These exceptions are specified in Sections 107, 108, and 109. They are paraphrased and summarized in the following paragraphs, out of sequence for purposes of clarity. Abridged text of Sections 106–109 may be found in appendix 4.1.

### Section 109—First Sale

Section 109 is the most straightforward as it applies to ILL practice. It contains a vital limitation on exclusive rights—the "effect of transfer of particular copy or phonorecord"—and what is commonly referred to as the "First Sale Doctrine." This principle allows people to give books, CDs, and DVDs as gifts. It also allows libraries to purchase and lend copyrighted works. It allows individuals and institutions to hold book sales. The owner of the copyrighted work is free to give it away or to loan, resell, discard, mutilate, or destroy it. A vital and frequently misunderstood distinction is that the ownership applies to the work as a physical item, not the intellectual content contained within it. Section 109 does not apply to works licensed by contract (see the section "ILL of Licensed Electronic Journals" later in this chapter).

### Section 108—Reproduction by Libraries and Archives

Section 108 contains "limitations on exclusive rights: reproduction by libraries and archives." Within limitations, this part of the law allows ILL departments to make, send, and receive copies of works. These copies can be for individual patrons, for other libraries, or for preservation, providing they conform to certain conditions. These rights can even apply to copies of an entire work or to substantial portions, if it has been determined, after a "reasonable investigation," that a copy cannot be obtained at a fair price or if the copyright holder has alerted the Register of Copyrights that the work is no longer being marketed.[3] Other conditions include the following:

1. To use Section 108, libraries must be eligible. Eligible libraries are those whose collections are open to the public, available not just to affiliated researchers but also to outside researchers.
2. Reproductions and their distribution must be on a cost-recovery basis only, not for direct or indirect commercial gain.
3. For a library user, the library or archive can copy one article from a periodical issue or a portion of another type of copyrighted work, such as a book chapter.
4. The copied work must include the copyright notice that appears on the work, or if that is absent or cannot be located, a notice must be included stating that the work may be protected by copyright.
5. The copy must become the property of the user.
6. The library or archives must have no notice that the copy would be used for any purpose other than private study, scholarship, or research.
7. The library or archives must display prominently, at the place where orders are accepted, and include on its order form, the following prescribed warning of copyright:

NOTICE

WARNING CONCERNING COPYRIGHT RESTRICTIONS

The copyright law of the United States (Title 17, United States Code) governs the making of photocopies or other reproductions of copyrighted material.

Under certain conditions specified in the law, libraries and archives are authorized to furnish a photocopy or other reproduction. One of these specific conditions is that the photocopy or reproduction is not to be "used for any purpose other than private study, scholarship, or research." If a user makes a request for, or later uses, a photocopy or reproduction for purposes in excess of "fair use," that user may be liable for copyright infringement.

This institution reserves the right to refuse to accept a copying order if, in its judgment, fulfillment of the order would involve violation of copyright law.

8. The copying must not be systematic; thus, this part of the law extends to copying and distribution of a single copy of the same material on separate occasions, but does not apply to related copying or distribution of multiple copies of the same material, whether made on one occasion or over a period of time.
9. Interlibrary loan arrangements such as consortial reciprocal agreements must not make copies in such "aggregate quantities" as to "substitute for a subscription to or purchase of" copyrighted works—Section 108(g)(2).
10. The rights of reproduction and distribution under this section do not apply to musical works (e.g., sheet music or recording of a musical performance), a pictorial, graphic or sculptural work, or a motion picture or other audiovisual work other than an audiovisual work dealing with news. Works published as adjuncts to articles or chapters such as illustrations, diagrams, charts, tables, photographs, and the like are the exception to this rule; they may be copied along with the rest of the work.

## CONTU Guidelines

### *CONTU*

Because the law itself is vague, Congress established the National Commission on New Technological Uses of Copyright Works, also known as CONTU, to develop more specific guidelines and to help define the "aggregate quantities" that could potentially "substitute for a subscription to or purchase of" copyrighted works. CONTU operated during the development and passage of the Copyright Act of 1976, between 1975 and 1978, and on July 31, 1978, it issued its Final Report. Chaired by Stanley H. Fuld (1903–2003), who served as Chief Judge of the New York Court of Appeals from 1967 through 1973, this diverse group had expertise in law, librarianship, education, and publishing.[4] Chapter 4 of the CONTU report, "Machine Reproduction—Photocopying," outlines the recommended interpretation of the law used in ILL practice today.[5] At that time, photocopiers were the newest technology. For copies reproduced in digital format, as is commonplace today, digital copies must not be distributed outside the library or made available to the public outside the premises of the library.[6] (See "Electronic Delivery" later in this chapter.)

*The "Suggestion of Five"*

The CONTU Final Report asserts that six or more copies of a recently published work could substitute for a subscription. "Recently published" is defined by CONTU as "within five years prior to the date of the [ILL] request." Thus, five copies from any single journal title requested within five years of the publication date of the work are considered to be within the so-called Suggestion of Five, also known as the Rule of Five or the 5/5 Rule. Copying of articles published more than five years after the date of the ILL request does not fall under Section 108, but may fall under Section 107.

For a very concrete example of the Suggestion of Five, over the course of the calendar year 2007, a library could have borrowed for any of its patrons the following five articles, just once each, appearing within the past five years of publication of the *Journal of Academic Librarianship*, while remaining within the Suggestion of Five:

1. Volume 32, Issue 3, May 2006, pages 251–58
2. Volume 30, Issue 2, March 2004, pages 132–35
3. Volume 33, Issue 4, July 2007, pages 462–77
4. Volume 31, Issue 1, January 2005, pages 46–53
5. Volume 32, Issue 1, January 2006, pages 69–78

However, once a sixth article is borrowed and filled (e.g., Volume 31, Issue 4, July 2005, pages 317–23), this action is defined by CONTU as potentially beginning to substitute for a subscription. To request that sixth article, the borrowing library must seek another source. Alternatives may include, but are not limited to, the following:

1. Borrow the sixth article from another library, and pay a copyright fee to the publisher, through the Copyright Clearance Center (discussed later in this chapter).
2. Deny or refuse the ILL order to its patron because the title is "closed" for the rest of the calendar year, suggesting the user place the request at the beginning of the next calendar year if still needed.
3. Start a subscription to the journal.
4. Purchase the article from a commercial document delivery vendor.
5. Purchase the article directly from the publisher on behalf of the patron.
6. Refer patrons to a nearby library with the title in its holdings.

The designation of "calendar year" can be confusing. The following example helps illustrate this concept. If a library receives an ILL borrowing request in September 2007 for an article published in the July–August 2002 issue of the *Journal of Academic Librarianship,* the publication date falls just outside the five years preceding the ILL request date; therefore, this request would fall outside the Suggestion of Five. Nevertheless, many libraries choose simply to include the remainder of the calendar year in their calculations.

When placing an ILL request for a photocopy, the borrowing library must indicate whether it complies with CONTU guidelines. This notification is commonly done with the abbreviations CCG or CCL. CCG is used for articles borrowed under the Suggestion of Five and means the request "complies with copyright guidelines," in reference to the CONTU guidelines. CCL means the request "complies with other provisions of the copyright law" (i.e., Section 107). Many libraries use CCL to indicate requests ordered from commercial document delivery vendors that include royalties in their fees.[7]

Under CONTU, it is the responsibility of the borrowing library to maintain records of ILL requests, both filled and unfilled, that could fall under the Suggestion of Five. These records must be retained for three years. Specifically, CONTU requires the borrowing library to maintain these records "until the end of the third complete calendar year after the end of the calendar year in which the respective request shall have been made."[8] In other words, ILL requests dated and filled between January 2003 and December 2003 may be discarded after December 2006. Electronic records are perfectly acceptable.

Although guidelines, including the CONTU guidelines, are not law, they are well established, and most ILL practitioners use them as an upper limit. However, a use beyond the CONTU Suggestion of Five might indeed pass the four-factor test and fall on the side of fair use. This decision must be made carefully on a case-by-case basis and according to local policy (see "Section 107—Fair Use" later in this chapter).

### Borrower Responsibilities and Options

The decision by a library about whether to subscribe to a journal is out of the scope of this chapter. However, acquisitions staff and ILL practitioners should work closely with one another to ensure that royalty fees, as well as the more hidden ILL transaction costs, do not exceed the price of a subscription and to ensure that collections are managed so that patrons' needs are met. Once a subscription to a journal title is started, the library can begin to borrow recent articles freely from it.

The Copyright Clearance Center (CCC; www.copyright.com) opened for business in 1978. It was organized by authors, publishers, and content users in response to a suggestion of Congress preceding the Copyright Act of 1976. Most publishers enable easy royalty payments for ILL transactions through CCC. Although their rationale is not known, some publishers do not participate in CCC. Frequently, commercial document delivery vendors, who pay publishers' royalties to provide articles, have arrangements with non-CCC publishers. Additionally, it has become much easier to purchase articles from publishers as publishers have begun to make individual articles available for immediate electronic download. It is hoped that outright denials of ILL requests are relatively rare due to alternate means of obtaining published works.

The CCL designation should be used for materials that are on order but not yet received by the library as well as for items currently unavailable, such as those at the bindery or in transit to off-site storage locations. However, what about articles from electronic journals that are currently embargoed? These requests should fall under the Suggestion of Five, and CCG should be used. Appropriate royalties should be paid as with any journal without a current subscription, as these items are neither currently owned nor yet paid for.[9]

### Section 107—Fair Use

Section 107 describes the popular concept of fair use. Fair use is a defense that can be used in court against allegations of copyright infringement. Courts consider the following four factors:

1. The **purpose and character of the use,** including whether such use is of a commercial nature or is for nonprofit educational purposes
2. The **nature of the copyrighted work**
3. The **amount and substantiality of the portion used** in relation to the copyrighted work as a whole
4. The **effect of the use upon the potential market** for or value of the copyrighted work

Although an exhaustive discussion of the concept of fair use is well beyond the scope of this chapter, ILL practitioners should familiarize themselves with this important part of the law. Table 4.1, inspired by Kenneth Crews's Fair Use Checklist, helps illustrate how the four factors are considered by courts.

## LENDER RESPONSIBILITIES

Although lending libraries are not obliged to keep records for copyright purposes, most do so for statistical purposes. Lenders have a few obligations when it comes to responsibility for copyright compliance.

Lending libraries need to ensure that photocopy requests have indicated compliance with either CONTU guidelines (CCG) or another part of the copyright law (CCL), as discussed earlier. Lending libraries are obliged to return to the borrowing library requests that are missing this information rather than filling them.

Lenders need to reproduce the copyright notice that appears on the work, along with the work itself. This requirement complies with modifications made to Section 108 by provisions in the Digital Millennium Copyright Act (DMCA) and in the Sonny Bono Copyright Term Extension Act of 1998. Most scholarly journal articles contain complete copyright information on at least the first page of the article itself. For older works, lenders may need to search for it, commonly in the front matter of the work. If no copyright notice can be found on the work, the lending library must include a notice similar to those that libraries used before the law changed.[10] This requirement can mean keeping the old-fashioned, ubiquitous, inky copyright stamp adjacent to most ILL photocopiers. In the case of electronic document delivery, however, the copyright notice is automatically included with delivery.

Lending libraries also need to have a good working knowledge of the limitations on borrowing libraries. Any lending request that appears to break limitations set by CONTU or by Fair Use may be refused and returned to the borrower. Borrowers should indicate if permission to copy has been obtained through the Copyright Clearance Center or the publisher or otherwise provide information to the lender for exceptional requests.

**Table 4.1** Fair Use Checklist

| | **Favoring Fair Use** | **Opposing Fair Use** |
|---|---|---|
| **Purpose and character of the use** | Not-for-profit, educational, news reporting, criticism, parody | For-profit, commercial, entertainment, bad-faith use |
| **Nature of the copyrighted work** | Published, factual work | Unpublished or highly creative work |
| **Amount and substantiality of the portion used** | Small quantity, appropriate portion | Large portion or copy of the "heart" of the work |
| **Effect of the use upon the potential market for or value of the work** | Lawful purchase or acquisition of work, no significant effect on the market, no licensing mechanism, few copies made | Could replace a sale, harm to market, distributed widely, easy and affordable permissions system, available, long-term use, many copies made |

Source: Adapted from Kenny Crews's Fair Use Checklist, http://copyright.columbia.edu/copyright/fair-use/fair-use-checklist/.

Finally, lending libraries need to know what their licenses for electronic journals permit with regard to ILL. Electronic journal licenses can range from disallowing any form of ILL to permitting full electronic document delivery. Frequently, licenses permit lending but only by paper printout. If your library has such licenses, it would be beneficial to renegotiate them so that they match current technology and practice in order to comply with turnaround time agreements and modern electronic document delivery technologies.

## ELECTRONIC DELIVERY

Paper copies are becoming increasingly obsolete. Most libraries deliver documents electronically, whether to their own patrons or to borrowing libraries. Borrowing libraries prefer to receive electronic copies. Naturally, this practice has possible copyright implications. The lending library must make a copy in order to send it to the borrowing library. However, this copy is deleted once it is received by the borrowing library. This procedure is parallel to the single (paper) copy becoming the property of the user, as specified by Section 108. On the borrowing side, documents are frequently posted on a password-protected website. The patron is normally limited to access within a specified time frame or limited to a set number of "views" of the document or both. However, the document can be printed or saved by the patron; thus, the single copy becomes the property of the user. In compliance with Section 108, libraries must not save copies of documents scanned for delivery to other libraries or provided for their patrons by other libraries; this could be construed as substitution for a subscription.[11]

## ILL OF LICENSED ELECTRONIC JOURNALS

Increasingly, libraries license works—including electronic journals and electronic books—that formerly were purchased in print format.[12] Because these are licensed works, they are subject to the terms of the license agreements, which fall under state contract law and not under copyright law, which is federal law. The contract's provisions determine which state's law applies.[13]

When libraries first began to acquire licensed works, many licenses did not permit ILL. Over time, licenses forbidding or severely restricting ILL would have a cumulative, deleterious effect on ILL as a whole. Increasingly, however, publishers, aggregators, and other providers are allowing ILL to some extent. In fact, according to studies conducted by the New York State–based IDS Project, less than 15 percent of licenses examined prohibited ILL under any circumstances.[14] However, licenses may specify how ILL is conducted, which can fall into a variety of permutations. Among them are "print ILL only" or "must print out a copy before scanning for electronic delivery." Although filling ILL requests directly from the electronic file is sometimes prohibited, many licenses allow direct electronic document delivery. Some licenses are silent regarding ILL. Many libraries assume tacit permission; others assume ILL is forbidden unless mentioned and specified. Collections of model licenses are being developed. Two such projects are NISO's SERU (Shared E-Resource Understanding; www.niso.org/workrooms/seru/) and Yale's Liblicense Model License Agreement (LMLA; www.library.yale.edu/~llicense/index.shtml). Library organizations offer negotiation workshops, and books and journal articles offer acquisitions staff assistance. Ideally, licenses should be negotiated (and in some cases renegotiated) so that any ILL process specified in the contract falls in line with the ILL department's preferred, most efficient workflow.

Janet Brennan Croft describes three approaches typically used by ILL practitioners when faced with license contracts: (1) the avoidance approach, in which ILL departments lend nothing simply because the resource happens to be electronic; (2) the reactive approach, in which files are maintained on which resources permit lending and how that lending must be conducted; and (3) the proactive approach, in which licenses are negotiated with ILL permissions.[15] Ideally, libraries would refuse to purchase a product that did not include ILL rights in the contract; however, practically, this approach might exclude necessary products from a library's collection. ARL's 1999 SPEC Kit on licenses indicated that 25 percent of libraries required ILL rights in the contract before signing it; this percentage is likely greater today.[16] Georgia Harper advises librarians, "Very rarely do vendors refuse to negotiate their terms."[17]

Finally, ILL practitioners, along with acquisitions staff and catalogers, should find a way to indicate license status so that lending staff know how to proceed when faced with a request from an electronic resource. Several vendors currently offer a wide variety of electronic resource management (ERM) products that assist not just ILL departments but other areas of the library as well. Open source ERM systems are also an option. Ideally, license codes such as the ones used by the IDS Project might someday be used in conjunction with ILL systems to indicate license requirements for lending requests and to simply deflect requests for (the few) sources from which ILL is not permitted.

### NONBOOK FORMATS

Generally, materials in nonbook format (CDs, DVDs, VHS tapes, and other multimedia formats) fall under Section 109 and may be borrowed and loaned under the First Sale Doctrine. However, in some cases, multimedia materials are licensed to libraries rather than sold. These licenses may carry restrictions on lending, especially to outside institutions, and especially in school settings.[18] As with other licensed works such as electronic journals, ILL practitioners should work with their acquisitions personnel to negotiate for ILL rights if possible and to ensure compliance with contract terms.

### INTERNATIONAL COPYRIGHT ISSUES

"The Convention for the Protection of Literary and Artistic Works" was signed in Berne, Switzerland, on September 9, 1886 (www.wipo.int/treaties/en/ip/berne/index.html). Otherwise known as the Berne Convention, this document supports international ILL. In 1988, the United States joined the Berne Convention, and all members of the European Union are also current signatories. Article 9, Right of Reproduction, states: "It shall be a matter for legislation in the countries of the Union to permit the reproduction of such works in certain special cases, provided that such reproduction does not conflict with a normal exploitation of the work and does not unreasonably prejudice the legitimate interests of the author." In order to conform to the Berne Convention standards, countries had to standardize some of their intellectual property laws. This work is still unfinished, and many countries' laws only partially conform.[19]

IFLA's International Resource Sharing and Document Delivery: Principles and Guidelines for Procedure, first agreed to by IFLA in 1954, was revised in February 2009 (www.ifla.org/files/docdel/documents/international-lending-en.pdf). It contains eight principles and guidelines; copyright is number six. It advises: "Due regard must be given to the copyright laws of the supplying country. While material requested on international ILL may often fall within 'fair use' or 'fair dealing' provisions, responsibility rests with the supplying library to inform the requesting library of any copyright restrictions which might apply." It continues in sections:

> 6.2. Each supplying library should be aware of, and work within, the copyright laws of its own country. In addition, the supplying library should ensure that any relevant copyright information is made available and communicated to requesting libraries.
>
> 6.3. Lending, and limited copying for purposes such as education, research or private study, are usually exceptions within national copyright legislation. The supplying library should inform the requesting library of these exceptions.
>
> 6.4. The requesting library should pay due regard to the copyright laws of the supplying library's country.
>
> 6.5. Each supplying library must abide by any licenses agreed to by their organisation, which may place some restrictions on the use of electronic resources for ILL transactions.

This document also refers to the IFLA Position on Copyright in the Digital Environment (revised January 25, 2001), which asserts that "digital is not different." It affirms the rights supported by the Berne Convention and treaties by the World Intellectual Property Organisation (WIPO). It states, "Contractual provisions, for example within licensing agreements, should not override reasonable lending of electronic resources by library and information staff" (http://archive.ifla.org/V/press/copydig.htm).

Despite harmonization efforts, Canadian libraries, for example, cannot deliver documents electronically to users. Section 30.2(5) of the Canadian Copyright Act states: "The copy given to the patron must not be in digital form."[20] As Canadian libraries continue to lobby their government for changes to allow electronic delivery, the Canada Institute for Scientific and Technical Information (CISTI) worked with CCC to license the right to provide electronic delivery for most journal titles.[21] Although ILL between countries is clearly encouraged, differences in copyright laws between countries are likely to continue to affect efficient ILL practice, at least in minor ways. The ILL practitioner can cope by establishing good working relationships with international libraries.

## APPENDIX 4.1

### *Abridged Full Text of United States Copyright Law, Title 17, Sections 106–109*

Complete text may be found at www.copyright.gov/title17/.

*§ 106 · Exclusive rights in copyrighted works*

Subject to sections 107 through 122, the owner of copyright under this title has the exclusive rights to do and to authorize any of the following:

(1) to reproduce the copyrighted work in copies or phonorecords;
(2) to prepare derivative works based upon the copyrighted work;
(3) to distribute copies or phonorecords of the copyrighted work to the public by sale or other transfer of ownership, or by rental, lease, or lending;
(4) in the case of literary, musical, dramatic, and choreographic works, pantomimes, and motion pictures and other audiovisual works, to perform the copyrighted work publicly;
(5) in the case of literary, musical, dramatic, and choreographic works, pantomimes, and pictorial, graphic, or sculptural works, including the individual images of a motion picture or other audiovisual work, to display the copyrighted work publicly; and
(6) in the case of sound recordings, to perform the copyrighted work publicly by means of a digital audio transmission.

*§ 107 · Limitations on exclusive rights: Fair use*

Notwithstanding the provisions of sections 106 and 106A, the fair use of a copyrighted work, including such use by reproduction in copies or phonorecords or by any other means specified by that section, for purposes such as criticism, comment, news reporting, teaching (including multiple copies for classroom use), scholarship, or research, is not an infringement of copyright. In determining whether the use made of a work in any particular case is a fair use the factors to be considered shall include—

(1) the purpose and character of the use, including whether such use is of a commercial nature or is for nonprofit educational purposes;
(2) the nature of the copyrighted work;
(3) the amount and substantiality of the portion used in relation to the copyrighted work as a whole; and

(4) the effect of the use upon the potential market for or value of the copyrighted work.

The fact that a work is unpublished shall not itself bar a finding of fair use if such finding is made upon consideration of all the above factors.

*§ 108 · Limitations on exclusive rights:*

Reproduction by libraries and archives

(a) Except as otherwise provided in this title and notwithstanding the provisions of section 106, it is not an infringement of copyright for a library or archives, or any of its employees acting within the scope of their employment, to reproduce no more than one copy or phonorecord of a work, except as provided in subsections (b) and (c), or to distribute such copy or phonorecord, under the conditions specified by this section, if—
  (1) the reproduction or distribution is made without any purpose of direct or indirect commercial advantage;
  (2) the collections of the library or archives are (i) open to the public, or (ii) available not only to researchers affiliated with the library or archives or with the institution of which it is a part, but also to other persons doing research in a specialized field; and
  (3) the reproduction or distribution of the work includes a notice of copyright that appears on the copy or phonorecord that is reproduced under the provisions of this section, or includes a legend stating that the work may be protected by copyright if no such notice can be found on the copy or phonorecord that is reproduced under the provisions of this section.

(b) The rights of reproduction and distribution under this section apply to three copies or phonorecords of an unpublished work duplicated solely for purposes of preservation and security or for deposit for research use in another library or archives of the type described by clause (2) of subsection (a), if—
  (1) the copy or phonorecord reproduced is currently in the collections of the library or archives; and
  (2) any such copy or phonorecord that is reproduced in digital format is not otherwise distributed in that format and is not made available to the public in that format outside the premises of the library or archives.

(c) The right of reproduction under this section applies to three copies or phonorecords of a published work duplicated solely for the purpose of replacement of a copy or phonorecord that is damaged, deteriorating, lost, or stolen, or if the existing format in which the work is stored has become obsolete, if—
  (1) the library or archives has, after a reasonable effort, determined that an unused replacement cannot be obtained at a fair price; and
  (2) any such copy or phonorecord that is reproduced in digital format is not made available to the public in that format outside the premises of the library or archives in lawful possession of such copy.

For purposes of this subsection, a format shall be considered obsolete if the machine or device necessary to render perceptible a work stored in that format is no longer manufactured or is no longer reasonably available in the commercial marketplace.

(d) The rights of reproduction and distribution under this section apply to a copy, made from the collection of a library or archives where the user makes his or her request or from that of another library or archives, of no more than one article or other contribution to a copyrighted collection or periodical issue, or to a copy or phonorecord of a small part of any other copyrighted work, if—

(1) the copy or phonorecord becomes the property of the user, and the library or archives has had no notice that the copy or phonorecord would be used for any purpose other than private study, scholarship, or research; and

(2) the library or archives displays prominently, at the place where orders are accepted, and includes on its order form, a warning of copyright in accordance with requirements that the Register of Copyrights shall prescribe by regulation.

(e) The rights of reproduction and distribution under this section apply to the entire work, or to a substantial part of it, made from the collection of a library or archives where the user makes his or her request or from that of another library or archives, if the library or archives has first determined, on the basis of a reasonable investigation, that a copy or phonorecord of the copyrighted work cannot be obtained at a fair price, if—

(1) the copy or phonorecord becomes the property of the user, and the library or archives has had no notice that the copy or phonorecord would be used for any purpose other than private study, scholarship, or research; and

(2) the library or archives displays prominently, at the place where orders are accepted, and includes on its order form, a warning of copyright in accordance with requirements that the Register of Copyrights shall prescribe by regulation.

(f) Nothing in this section—

(1) shall be construed to impose liability for copyright infringement upon a library or archives or its employees for the unsupervised use of reproducing equipment located on its premises: Provided, That such equipment displays a notice that the making of a copy may be subject to the copyright law;

(2) excuses a person who uses such reproducing equipment or who requests a copy or phonorecord under subsection (d) from liability for copyright infringement for any such act, or for any later use of such copy or phonorecord, if it exceeds fair use as provided by section 107;

(3) shall be construed to limit the reproduction and distribution by lending of a limited number of copies and excerpts by a library or archives of an audiovisual news program, subject to clauses (1), (2), and (3) of subsection (a); or

(4) in any way affects the right of fair use as provided by section 107, or any contractual obligations assumed at any time by the library or archives when it obtained a copy or phonorecord of a work in its collections.

(g) The rights of reproduction and distribution under this section extend to the isolated and unrelated reproduction or distribution of a single copy or phonorecord of the same material on separate occasions, but do not extend to cases where the library or archives, or its employee—

(1) is aware or has substantial reason to believe that it is engaging in the related or concerted reproduction or distribution of multiple copies or phonorecords of the same material, whether made on one occasion or over a period of time, and whether intended for aggregate use by one or more individuals or for separate use by the individual members of a group; or

(2) engages in the systematic reproduction or distribution of single or multiple

copies or phonorecords of material described in subsection (d): Provided, That nothing in this clause prevents a library or archives from participating in interlibrary arrangements that do not have, as their purpose or effect, that the library or archives receiving such copies or phonorecords for distribution does so in such aggregate quantities as to substitute for a subscription to or purchase of such work.

(h)

(1) For purposes of this section, during the last 20 years of any term of copyright of a published work, a library or archives, including a nonprofit educational institution that functions as such, may reproduce, distribute, display, or perform in facsimile or digital form a copy or phonorecord of such work, or portions thereof, for purposes of preservation, scholarship, or research, if such library or archives has first determined, on the basis of a reasonable investigation, that none of the conditions set forth in subparagraphs (A), (B), and (C) of paragraph (2) apply.

(2) No reproduction, distribution, display, or performance is authorized under this subsection if—

(A) the work is subject to normal commercial exploitation;

(B) a copy or phonorecord of the work can be obtained at a reasonable price; or

(C) the copyright owner or its agent provides notice pursuant to regulations promulgated by the Register of Copyrights that either of the conditions set forth in subparagraphs (A) and (B) applies.

(3) The exemption provided in this subsection does not apply to any subsequent uses by users other than such library or archives.

(i) The rights of reproduction and distribution under this section do not apply to a musical work, a pictorial, graphic or sculptural work, or a motion picture or other audiovisual work other than an audiovisual work dealing with news, except that no such limitation shall apply with respect to rights granted by subsections (b), (c), and (h), or with respect to pictorial or graphic works published as illustrations, diagrams, or similar adjuncts to works of which copies are reproduced or distributed in accordance with subsections (d) and (e).

*§ 109 · Limitations on exclusive rights:*

Effect of transfer of particular copy or phonorecord

(a) Notwithstanding the provisions of section 106(3), the owner of a particular copy or phonorecord lawfully made under this title, or any person authorized by such owner, is entitled, without the authority of the copyright owner, to sell or otherwise dispose of the possession of that copy or phonorecord. Notwithstanding the preceding sentence, copies or phonorecords of works subject to restored copyright under section 104A that are manufactured before the date of restoration of copyright or, with respect to reliance parties, before publication or service of notice under section 104A(e), may be sold or otherwise disposed of without the authorization of the owner of the restored copyright for purposes of direct or indirect commercial advantage only during the 12-month period beginning on—

(1) the date of the publication in the *Federal Register* of the notice of intent filed with the Copyright Office under section 104A(d)(2)(A), or

(2) the date of the receipt of actual notice served under section 104A(d)(2)(B), whichever occurs first.

(b)

(1)

(A) Notwithstanding the provisions of subsection (a), unless authorized by the owners of copyright in the sound recording or the owner of copyright in a computer program (including any tape, disk, or other medium embodying such program), and in the case of a sound recording in the musical works embodied therein, neither the owner of a particular phonorecord nor any person in possession of a particular copy of a computer program (including any tape, disk, or other medium embodying such program), may, for the purposes of direct or indirect commercial advantage, dispose of, or authorize the disposal of, the possession of that phonorecord or computer program (including any tape, disk, or other medium embodying such program) by rental, lease, or lending, or by any other act or practice in the nature of rental, lease, or lending. Nothing in the preceding sentence shall apply to the rental, lease, or lending of a phonorecord for nonprofit purposes by a nonprofit library or nonprofit educational institution.

The transfer of possession of a lawfully made copy of a computer program by a nonprofit educational institution to another nonprofit educational institution or to faculty, staff, and students does not constitute rental, lease, or lending for direct or indirect commercial purposes under this subsection.

(B) This subsection does not apply to—

(i) a computer program which is embodied in a machine or product and which cannot be copied during the ordinary operation or use of the machine or product; or

(ii) a computer program embodied in or used in conjunction with a limited purpose computer that is designed for playing video games and may be designed for other purposes.

(C) Nothing in this subsection affects any provision of chapter 9 of this title.

(2)

(A) Nothing in this subsection shall apply to the lending of a computer program for nonprofit purposes by a nonprofit library, if each copy of a computer program which is lent by such library has affixed to the packaging containing the program a warning of copyright in accordance with requirements that the Register of Copyrights shall prescribe by regulation.

(B) Not later than three years after the date of the enactment of the Computer Software Rental Amendments Act of 1990, and at such times thereafter as the Register of Copyrights considers appropriate, the Register of Copyrights, after consultation with representatives of copyright owners and librarians, shall submit to the Congress a report stating whether this paragraph has achieved its intended purpose of maintaining the integrity of the copyright system while providing nonprofit libraries the capability to fulfill their function. Such report shall advise the Congress as to any information or recommendations that the Register of Copyrights considers necessary to carry out the purposes of this subsection.

(3) Nothing in this subsection shall affect any provision of the antitrust laws. For purposes of the preceding sentence, "antitrust laws" has the meaning given that term in the first section of the Clayton Act and includes section 5 of the Federal Trade Commission Act to the extent that section relates to unfair methods of competition.

(4) Any person who distributes a phonorecord or a copy of a computer program (including any tape, disk, or other medium embodying such program) in violation of paragraph (1) is an infringer of copyright under section 501 of this title and is subject to the remedies set forth in sections 502, 503, 504, and 505. Such violation shall not be a criminal offense under section 506 or cause such person to be subject to the criminal penalties set forth in section 2319 of title 18.

(c) Notwithstanding the provisions of section 106(5), the owner of a particular copy lawfully made under this title, or any person authorized by such owner, is entitled, without the authority of the copyright owner, to display that copy publicly, either directly or by the projection of no more than one image at a time, to viewers present at the place where the copy is located.

(d) The privileges prescribed by subsections (a) and (c) do not, unless authorized by the copyright owner, extend to any person who has acquired possession of the copy or phonorecord from the copyright owner, by rental, lease, loan, or otherwise, without acquiring ownership of it.

(e) Notwithstanding the provisions of sections 106(4) and 106(5), in the case of an electronic audiovisual game intended for use in coin-operated equipment, the owner of a particular copy of such a game lawfully made under this title, is entitled, without the authority of the copyright owner of the game, to publicly perform or display that game in coin-operated equipment, except that this subsection shall not apply to any work of authorship embodied in the audiovisual game if the copyright owner of the electronic audiovisual game is not also the copyright owner of the work of authorship.

## NOTES

1. Lee Andrew Hilyer, "Copyright in the Interlibrary Loan Department," *Interlibrary Loan and Document Delivery: Best Practices for Operating and Managing Interlibrary Loan Services in All Libraries* (New York: Haworth Press, 2006), 53–64. Simultaneously published in *Journal of Interlibrary Loan, Document Delivery, and Electronic Reserve* 16, no. 1–2 (2006).
2. American Library Association, Interlibrary Loans: ALA Library Fact Sheet Number 8, www.ala.org/ala/professionalresources/libfactsheets/alalibraryfactsheet08.cfm.
3. Carrie Russell, *Complete Copyright: An Everyday Guide for Librarians* (Chicago: American Library Association, 1994).
4. *New York Times*, Deaths: Judge Stanley H. Fuld, July 27, 2003, www.nytimes.com/2003/07/27/classified/paid-notice-deaths-fuld-judge-stanley-h.html?pagewanted=1.
5. CONTU (National Commission on New Technological Uses of Copyright Works), Final Report of the National Commission on New Technological Uses of Copyright Works, July 31, 1978, Library of Congress, Washington, DC, 1979, 47–48, http://digital-law-online.info/CONTU/PDF/index.html.
6. Russell, *Complete Copyright.*
7. Hilyer, "Copyright in the Interlibrary Loan Department," 53–64.
8. CONTU, 55.

9. Laura Gasaway, "Questions and Answers: Copyright Column," *Against the Grain* 17, no. 6 (2005): 61-62.
10. Georgia Harper, Copyright Crash Course: Copyright in the Library; Interlibrary Loan, www.utsystem.edu/ogc/intellectualproperty/l-108g.htm.
11. Janet Brennan Croft, "Interlibrary Loan and Licensing: Tools for Proactive Contract Management," in *Licensing in Libraries: Practical and Ethical Aspects,* ed. Karen Rupp-Serrano, 41–53 (New York: Haworth Press, 2005). Simultaneously published in *Journal of Library Administration* 42, no. 3–4 (2005): 41–53.
12. Harper, Copyright Crash Course.
13. Donna Nixon, "Copyright and Interlibrary Loan Rights," *Journal of Interlibrary Loan, Document Delivery and Information Supply* 13, no. 3 (2003): 69.
14. IDS Project (New York: SUNY Geneseo), www.idsproject.org/index.aspx.
15. Croft, "Interlibrary Loan and Licensing."
16. Ibid., 50.
17. Quoted in Croft, "Interlibrary Loan and Licensing," 51.
18. Carol Simpson, "Interlibrary Loan of Audiovisuals May Bring a Lawsuit," *Library Media Connection* 26, no. 5 (February 2008): 26–30.
19. Cristine Martins and Sophia Martins, "Electronic Copyright in a Shrinking World," *Computers in Libraries* 22, no. 5 (2002): 31.
20. Robert Tiessen, "Copyright's Effect on Interlibrary Loan in Canada and the United States," *Journal of Interlibrary Loan, Document Delivery and Electronic Reserve* 18, no. 1 (2007): 101–11.
21. Ibid., 104.

## BIBLIOGRAPHY


American Library Association. Interlibrary Loans. ALA Library Fact Sheet Number 8. www.ala.org/ala/professionalresources/libfactsheets/alalibraryfactsheet08.cfm.

CONTU (National Commission on New Technological Uses of Copyright Works). Final Report of the National Commission on New Technological Uses of Copyright Works, July 31, 1978. Washington, DC: Library of Congress, 1979. www.cni.org/docs/infopols/CONTU.html or http://digital-law-online.info/CONTU/PDF/index.html.

Crews, Kenneth. Fair Use Checklist. New York: Columbia University Libraries/Information Services, Copyright Advisory Office. http://copyright.columbia.edu/copyright/fair-use/fair-use-checklist/.

Croft, Janet Brennan. *Legal Solutions in Electronic Reserves and in the Electronic Delivery of Interlibrary Loan.* New York: Haworth Press, 2004. Simultaneously published in *Journal of Interlibrary Loan, Document Delivery and Information Supply* 14, no. 3 (2004).

———. "Interlibrary Loan and Licensing: Tools for Proactive Contract Management." In *Licensing in Libraries: Practical and Ethical Aspects,* edited by Karen Rupp-Serrano, 41–53. New York: Haworth Press, 2005. Simultaneously published in *Journal of Library Administration* 42, no. 3–4 (2005): 41–53.

Gasaway, Laura. "Questions and Answers: Copyright Column." *Against the Grain* 17, no. 6 (2005): 61–62.

Harper, Georgia. Copyright Crash Course: Copyright in the Library; Interlibrary Loan. www.utsystem.edu/ogc/intellectualproperty/l-108g.htm.

Hilyer, Lee Andrew. "Copyright in the Interlibrary Loan Department." *Interlibrary Loan and Document Delivery: Best Practices for Operating and Managing Interlibrary Loan Services in All Libraries.* New York: Haworth Press, 2006, 53–64. Simultaneously published in *Journal of Interlibrary Loan, Document Delivery and Electronic Reserve* 16, no. 1–2 (2006).

IDS Project. New York: SUNY Geneseo. www.idsproject.org/index.aspx.

Martins, Cristine, and Sophia Martins. "Electronic Copyright in a Shrinking World." *Computers in Libraries* 22, no. 5 (2002): 28–31.

*New York Times*. Deaths. Judge Stanley H. Fuld, July 27, 2003. www.nytimes.com/2003/07/27/classified/paid-notice-deaths-fuld-judge-stanley-h.html?pagewanted=1.

Nixon, Donna. "Copyright and Interlibrary Loan Rights." *Journal of Interlibrary Loan, Document Delivery and Information Supply* 13, no. 3 (2003): 55–89.

Russell, Carrie. *Complete Copyright: An Everyday Guide for Librarians*. Chicago: American Library Association, 1994.

Simpson, Carol. "Interlibrary Loan of Audiovisuals May Bring a Lawsuit." *Library Media Connection* 26, no. 5 (February 2008): 26–30.

Tiessen, Robert. "Copyright's Effect on Interlibrary Loan in Canada and the United States." *Journal of Interlibrary Loan, Document Delivery and Electronic Reserve* 18, no. 1 (2007): 101–11.

CHAPTER FIVE

# MANAGEMENT OF INTERLIBRARY LOAN

*Jennifer Kuehn*

MANAGING AN INTERLIBRARY loan unit requires the ability to manage change. Interlibrary loan is done very differently now than it was even a decade ago. Automation, the information landscape, users' expectations, and the tools we have at our disposal to meet patrons' needs have changed, and these changes have influenced interlibrary loan practice. As more libraries implemented automated ILL management systems, two functions that once took a great deal of time became unnecessary: keeping manual files and keying data. Freed from filing, ILL units have been able to make tremendous improvements in productivity and enhancements of the services they provide. The past two decades have also seen an increase in overall request volume.

An interlibrary loan office is a vibrant unit, working with and impacted by so many other functions of the library. As a public service, it works directly with patrons and relies on other units within the local library to be able to perform its work. One example of this interdependency with other library units is extensive use of the online catalog and integrated library system (ILS). Is there another unit in the library that searches the catalog as often as interlibrary loan? Interlibrary loan might be viewed as the library's biggest user of the catalog, possibly having more material checked out to it than to any single, local patron.

But how do we manage and advance the service we provide? The most important strategy is to look for opportunities to consider how something could be done a different way. Listen to what your patrons say and get involved professionally to learn what your peers are doing and why. Look at your own workflows. Consider what you are doing well to build on your strengths and review your weaknesses to see where you can improve. Consider your mission and develop goals with an understanding of the costs involved in meeting them. You may want to use the

Rethinking Resource Sharing initiative and its seven principles as a starting point and ask what you might do to reduce the barriers to service for users. The Rethinking Resource Sharing initiative (http://rethinkingresourcesharing.org/manifesto.html) aims to foster an updated framework of cooperation and collaboration and to encourage libraries to find new ways to serve their patrons as well as all potential users.

Interlibrary loan management almost always involves managing at least two distinct services: borrowing and lending. An interlibrary loan borrowing operation typically obtains specific items when a patron's needs aren't met by the local collection. Traditionally, this service has been provided by borrowing materials from other libraries, but the department may also obtain items in other ways. Increasingly, ILL units are directing patrons to available local print or online content, purchasing items for the collection on demand, purchasing an item that is given to the individual requestor to keep, or obtaining an item directly from an author, publisher, association, or cultural heritage organization. These varied approaches go beyond simply borrowing from other libraries to "get it" for the patron from whatever source can be found. Sometimes, ILL serves as a gatekeeper by determining by policy just how far the library will go to meet a patron's request. That's an area where the management of interlibrary loan both directs and reflects practice.

Management of a lending operation is the other side of the coin because we are serving other libraries' patrons with our collection. Borrowing can only be successful if there are lending libraries to fill requests. Even though there are more choices of sources in borrowing than simply requesting from another library, the sharing of resources between libraries continues to grow.

Our library community has embraced the idea that access complements ownership. Improving that access includes improving lending operations, which in turn allows us to confidently tell our patrons that we can get it for them, thereby meeting the raised user expectations in an environment of increased access. This chapter will explore five aspects of ILL management: the ILL environment, policy development, assessment, staffing and human resources, and working with other units in the library.

## THE ILL ENVIRONMENT

Managing an ILL unit requires careful consideration of the changes taking place in other library services. Additionally, keep in mind that other commercial services increase patrons' expectations for interlibrary service. Traditional library-to-library interlibrary loan is not the only option for patrons when something is unavailable locally. Internet booksellers are ubiquitous, and patrons may use multiple libraries (public libraries, for example, also serve college and university patrons). When a patron's own institution does not have something available, other resource-sharing services may exist that would be preferred to interlibrary loan, such as patron-initiated borrowing through a consortial catalog. Consortia of all kinds have been developed that enhance and streamline sharing among libraries, particularly for returnable materials. Examples of these cooperatives include I-Share in Illinois, OhioLINK in Ohio, MeLCat in Michigan, and Orbis Cascade's Summit in Washington State and Oregon. Some of these consortia consist of multiple library types enriching the assortment of material readily available for patrons through one union catalog. Despite the variety of potential suppliers, no one consortium, like no one library, has everything, so traditional interlibrary services are still needed.

Patrons' expectations have changed, too. The universe of what a patron can discover has greatly expanded, and patrons have come to expect levels of service for ease of requesting and speed of delivery that rarely existed a dozen years ago. If a user can request a book from other libraries within a state, monitor that it's been found and shipped, and know that it will likely arrive within a few days and be delivered to an office or preferred convenient library, that user may expect ILL to approximate the same process. With the growth of article citation databases and electronic journals, patrons see that it is possible to purchase an article directly from a publisher with a credit card, raising patrons' expectations of how quickly materials can be obtained.

As a manager for interlibrary services, you have many resources to support your work. In your own institution there are many people with whom you will want and need to interact, which will be discussed later in this chapter. But outside your library there are many colleagues for you to meet who are doing similar work in libraries not unlike yours. There are electronic discussion lists, journals, and conferences focused solely on interlibrary services and resource sharing. Within the American Library Association, STARS (Sharing and Transforming Access to Resources Section) is a section of RUSA (Reference and User Services Association) and brings together librarians and library staff members for activities at conferences and committee work throughout the year. If you subscribe to state or national interlibrary loan e-mail discussion groups, you can check the archives to see how a topic has been addressed in the past and then post questions. Another strategy for professional development is to find peers in your area and visit their "shop." Such visits not only foster collegial relationships but also help you reflect on what you might do differently in your environment. State, regional, and local library groups may also have interlibrary loan groups or be able to connect you to colleagues. Simply put, a best practice is to become a part of the interlibrary loan community. As people who share resources professionally, it is a community that willingly shares its knowledge, too.

## POLICY DEVELOPMENT

Interlibrary loan policy development requires looking at the departmental and library-wide environment, considering the mission of the library, and then aligning policies with service goals. A good place to start is by reviewing the Interlibrary Loan Code for the United States. The purpose of the code is to describe "the responsibilities of libraries to each other when requesting material for users."[1] The code has a long history as a guiding principle for interlibrary loan.

The U.S. Interlibrary Loan Code, first published in 1917 and adopted by the American Library Association in 1919, is designed to provide a code of behavior for requesting and supplying material within the United States. This code does not override individual or consortial agreements or regional or state codes that may be more liberal or more prescriptive. This national code is intended to provide guidelines for exchanges between libraries where no other agreement applies. The code is intended to be adopted voluntarily by U.S. libraries and is not enforced by an oversight body. However, as indicated later in this chapter, supplying libraries may suspend service to borrowing libraries that fail to comply with the provisions of this code.

In addition to the U.S. Interlibrary Loan Code, states, regions, or other library cooperatives may have policies or service expectations that should be reviewed.

**Table 5.1** Interlibrary Loan Policy Elements

| | Borrowing | Lending |
|---|---|---|
| Mission/Goal | X | X |
| Who is served | X | X |
| How requests can be made | X | X |
| Typical time for fulfillment—how long will it take? | X | X |
| Fees and methods of payment accepted | X | X |
| Limitations of service | X | X |
| Number of requests allowed per person | X | |
| Number of pieces loaned at one time | | X |
| Formats that are difficult to fill and will not be attempted | X | X |
| Formats that are difficult to fill but will be attempted | X | |
| Patron responsibilities | X | |
| Library responsibilities | | X |
| Delivery methods | X | X |
| Notification methods | X | |
| Length of loan, renewals | X | X |
| Lost material fees/procedures | X | X |
| Contact information | X | X |

Next, review your existing policies and any written statements that may already guide current practice. When examining policies, look at the who, what, where, how, and why of the service, both in the present and what it might be in the future, keeping in mind that interlibrary services can showcase a commitment to meeting patrons' needs. Generally speaking, policies do not vary greatly from library to library. Many libraries have similar policies with small differences reflecting goals, the need to limit costs, or the number of available staff. Some of the elements of interlibrary loan policies are illustrated in table 5.1, which shows that borrowing and lending policies are quite parallel.

### Whom Do You Serve?

In academic libraries, the primary clientele are usually faculty (including emeritus and visiting faculty), staff, and students. If you prohibit a specific type of user (e.g., undergraduates), it is not uncommon for the determined user to seek others to act as a proxy. Serving all without any distinction prevents this unnecessary ruse. Additional clientele that might be served include alumni, businesses, or patrons from the community who may or may not have a formal relationship with the institution. And although individuals might be the typical users, research work groups and projects can be served, too, usually with one person named for pickup and delivery. You will want to define your primary constituents but be open to considering others who might be your customers, too. Your institution's service philosophy and level of commitment to reaching out beyond the primary clientele may help guide your decision.

Public libraries typically serve local residents and other cardholding patrons, which may include businesses or groups such as book clubs. The public library serves people in all aspects of their lives, including personal interests, work-related needs, or lifelong learning pursuits. More often than in academic libraries, public libraries might ask the requestor to pay the fees associated with borrowing. School and corporate libraries also engage in resource-sharing activities, but special and corporate libraries may have fewer opportunities to partner with other libraries in terms of consortial catalogs, leaving traditional interlibrary loan as the model used to meet their clients' needs.

### What Will You Borrow? What Will It Cost?

After you have developed an overarching service goal, decide what you will do for your patrons. You can choose how far you'll go for a patron, how much you are willing to subsidize requests, or how much support you will provide for one patron over time or a research project. Setting service limits may be difficult, but it's easier to set by policy in advance than when a request comes in.

In addition to borrowing from another library, many options now exist for procuring an item for a patron. Resource discovery is easier for patrons, resulting in requests for material types that are new, different, and possibly not appropriate for loan. Ongoing review and updating of policies will be necessary as barriers to what can be obtained break down. For example, as it becomes easier to find a source, make requests, and pay for them internationally, it will be easier to extend borrowing practice to include international ILL. As you are able to ease restrictions on borrowing, it may also make sense to remove them in lending.

Your policy should also list the types of material that may be difficult or impossible to get through interlibrary loan. That list might include many types of materials: old, rare, items of high value, whole issues or volumes of serials, reference books, computer manuals, genealogy books, new publications or those in high demand, manuscripts, screenplays, scripts, scores, multivolume sets, phonorecords, media (e.g., VHS tapes, DVDs, CDs), and theses or dissertations. You might address how you will handle requests for things not yet published, as users frequently find works that are not yet available. Those requests could be canceled outright or referred to collection development staff.

It is important to distinguish between hard-to-get materials and what you won't even try to obtain. However, keep in mind that an increasing number of formerly rare material types can now be obtained, though it may require more work. Libraries are also more willing to borrow material that is already owned by the library but in use by another patron, in a noncirculating collection, or at the bindery. As interlibrary borrowing becomes faster, it may be quicker to borrow a copy from elsewhere rather than wait for the library's own copy to be returned through a recall or due date. This willingness to borrow more stems from how much easier it is to make requests as well as a trend toward longer due dates and more flexible circulation practices. Academic libraries are still debating whether textbooks should be borrowable. Some institutions consider textbook purchases to be part of the students' responsibility while others may be more willing to get whatever their patrons need. Academic libraries are also increasingly willing to subsidize recreational interests of their clientele, rather than just supporting scholarly interests, especially as it is often difficult to distinguish between the two. These issues should be addressed in your policy.

### How Do Users Place Requests? How Do Patrons Receive Requested Materials?

Determining which methods of requesting to allow requires balancing the needs of users, staff workload, and costs. You may allow requests from paper or online request forms, e-mail, telephone, or WorldCat or via OpenURL from article databases. However, streamlining request processes can reduce errors and workload, while still providing acceptable service to users. For example, being able to accept requests over the telephone does not necessarily mean that the department should choose to make this a service option. Inform your patrons of the various methods by which to submit requests in a variety of places, especially at their point of discovery. It is also important to work with library administration to obtain support and understanding for the scope of service, and then share the final product with other library staff members who work directly with patrons (e.g., reference, instruction, and circulation units).

You may want to include a statement about patron responsibility for fines, late returns, damaged materials, or lost items, noting that failure to return materials on time may damage the relationship with other libraries and compromise the ability to borrow in the future. It is also important to note that the loan period is set by the lender. Patrons also need to know if you will renew and if so, for how long, your methods of delivery or pickup, and how patrons will be notified about the arrival of their request. Lee Hilyer provides a nice sample fee FAQ in his book.[2] Although patrons do not always read these policy statements, it is still a best practice to make the information available.

### How Long Will It Take? How Much Does It Cost the User?

Patrons typically ask two things about the service: How long will it take? and How much do I have to pay? The answer to "how long" may be unknown for any one request because we can't really predict the future, but giving a general or average answer is helpful to shape expectations. Although patrons may see increasingly faster turnaround time for articles because of electronic delivery, loans must be shipped and will often take longer to obtain.

Your library may subsidize the cost of providing interlibrary loan because of the library's philosophy that the service is a necessary extension of the collection to support users' needs. Other libraries may not have this luxury or may be forced to set limits. One option is to charge a flat fee to users for each request. Another option is to offer the service with the expectation that patrons will pay any lending or copyright fees associated with their request. Still other options are to charge in specific circumstances, such as for dissertations ordered on demand, materials requested but not picked up, or overdue fees. Some libraries ask for a maximum cost the patron is willing to pay, although such libraries try to get the material from free sources first. By asking the question upfront at the point where the user places the request, staff members do not have to contact the patron for permission to continue pursuing the request with lending libraries that charge. If any component of your service might require a payment from a user, make it clear in your written policies. Keep in mind, however, that collecting fees is not without cost for the library, both in staff time to manage the process and in bank fees associated with credit card or check payments.

### What about Lending Policies?

Although it is tempting to focus on your own patrons, it is important not to omit lending activities when creating or revising policies. Although the OCLC Policies Directory currently is the primary place to display this information for thousands of libraries, a lending website is a smart addition, particularly for high-volume lenders or for those with unique collections that may be sought after by libraries that do not utilize OCLC. Although not all borrowing libraries will see your lending website or look up your information in the OCLC Policies Directory, having it available and up to date makes you a better partner. You should answer the basic questions about your lending activities (the who, what, where, when, and how of your service) on a web page as well as in the OCLC Policies Directory. A lending web page can also be a good place to showcase unique services like digitizing on demand, maintaining an institutional repository of electronic theses and dissertations (ETDs), your willingness to copy or provide reference service from genealogy collections, or lending from special collections. University libraries should articulate their policy on lending theses or dissertations or both, particularly if purchasing copies from ProQuest is an alternative, because borrowing libraries may be unfamiliar with that option.

The most important element to include in your lending policy is basic contact information: library name, institution name, what you call your unit, address(es), e-mail, phone and fax numbers, hours, holiday closures, and the like. For larger units, make it clear who to contact for various services. Parallel to the information you provide in a borrowing policy, include the various methods by which you are willing to accept requests (e.g., by phone, fax, e-mail, WorldCat Resource Sharing, or web form). Outline the collections your unit will not loan at all. Some libraries are unable to loan bound serials, audiovisual material, government documents, or other unique collections. Explain the various delivery methods you use when loaning your materials and the shipping method you want borrowers to use when returning materials. You may have multiple methods of delivery for photocopies, including Odyssey, Ariel, fax, mail, as e-mail attachments, or posting the articles you lend on a server and allowing borrowing libraries to retrieve them from a link provided in an e-mail notification. For microforms or for multivolume sets of books, you might limit the number of pieces you will lend at one time on a single request in order to reduce possible loss or because of shipping cost considerations. Delivery services such as FedEx and UPS offer tracking and make loss less likely, so you might offer varying limits.

Describe your fee structure and the methods of payment accepted, including your fees and the process for replacing items that get lost in a transaction. Fees can be established to reduce demand, to offer pricing comparable to that of peer institutions, or to recover actual and indirect costs incurred for lending activities. If you are lending internationally, the International Federation of Library Associations and Institutions (IFLA) has a voucher system with reusable plastic payment cards (see http://archive.ifla.org/VI/2/p1/vouchers.htm). Libraries are encouraged, but not required, to accept one voucher as payment for a single loan or photocopy. The scheme reduces the need for invoices, bank fees, and loss of revenue through currency exchange. If you are willing to accept IFLA vouchers for payment, you then have them on hand when you need them for borrowing.

An increasing number of libraries are reconsidering the standard loan period. Lengthening the loan period may reduce the number of renewals requested and the workload that accompanies renewal processing. Some libraries also choose to extend the loan period and decline to grant renewals. An alternative workflow that some libraries employ is to convert lending requests into digitization-on-demand requests for materials in the public domain. The borrowing library pays for the digitization and the lending library fills the request but then makes the work freely available. If a library digitizes material, it is helpful to add the URL for the digital version to the OCLC cataloging record to assist in its discovery and use by others.

## ASSESSMENT

The Association of Research Libraries (ARL) has conducted three major studies that have provided important baseline data for interlibrary loan service evaluation. These studies developed instruments for measuring costs in order to make comparisons across institutions. In addition to cost data, the studies provide us with the best practices of high-performing libraries that can be adopted by others.

The first, a cost study, was done in 1992 as a joint project of ARL and the Research Libraries Group (RLG) and had seventy-six participants from the United States and Canada.[3] Researchers learned that staff costs accounted for 77 percent of total transaction cost (combined borrowing and lending). The second study was conducted in 1996 with 119 participants—ninety-seven research libraries and twenty-two college libraries from the Oberlin Group.[4] The results are broken out for the two library types for costs, fill rate, turnaround time, and user satisfaction. A series of best practices workshops followed this study as characteristics of high-performance borrowing and lending units were identified based on costs, turnaround time, and fill rates. The last study occurred in 2002 with seventy-two participants.[5] This most recent study provided an added focus on user-initiated and local document delivery services. It confirmed the success of user-initiated services and recommended moving toward that model.

Additional studies of many ILL operations that provide detailed statistics on many facets and trends of ILL include the Higher Education Interlibrary Loan Management Benchmarks study.[6] The survey sample of seventy-seven libraries included community colleges as well as colleges and universities, with detailed comments from individual libraries on such issues as workflow, budgeting, distance learning, shipping, and personnel. Through detailed profiles of nine institutions' interlibrary operations, *Profiles of Best Practices in Academic Interlibrary Loan* offers advice and recommendations for issues facing ILL managers in 2009.[7]

Managers of library services commonly ask, "What statistics should I keep and how can I evaluate our services?" As library service evaluation becomes more data-driven, it may prove even more valuable to track the volume and success of the service and ensure that the valuable work provided is recognized. Four typical methods are used to assess interlibrary services: fill rate, cost, turnaround time, and user studies. Fill rate and turnaround time are easiest to produce and document service trends more readily than user or cost studies, while user surveys might provide a richer, more contextual evaluation of the service. Although data do provide answers to questions that require counts, the context of those numbers and the trends illustrated by comparisons over time may be more important than a single point of data. It is useful to look for trends by comparing a statistic against the same statistic from a prior month or year or from the same month in the prior year. Are your numbers going up or down, and do you know why? If you are able to identify trends, you can predict future demand and determine the human and financial resources you will need for the service.

Basic statistics are generally kept monthly and compiled in an annual report. The most basic elements are requests received, requests filled, and requests not filled, perhaps separated by copies and loans, for both borrowing and lending. In any given month, however, some requests that are filled were placed the previous month. For example, a request filled in December may have been placed in November. Some management systems may report this differently, counting only the requests both made and filled in the same month.

**Table 5.2** Sample Monthly Request Activity Report

| | Total Requests Received | Requests Filled | Requests Unfilled | Percentage Filled | Percentage Unfilled |
|---|---|---|---|---|---|
| Photocopies | | | | | |
| Loans | | | | | |

**Table 5.3** Sample Yearly Compilation

| | Total Requests Received | Total Requests Filled | Total Requests Unfilled | Percentage Filled | Percentage Unfilled |
|---|---|---|---|---|---|
| January | | | | | |
| February | | | | | |
| March | | | | | |

Both borrowing and lending activities may report the same basic types of statistics as shown in table 5.2. As illustrated in table 5.3, you can adapt this report to reflect yearly totals, often broken down by month, either aggregated to include loans and photocopies or limited to just one type of request.

Additional levels of statistics might also be warranted, such as those required by state, consortial, or reciprocal partnerships. You may want to know how much of the borrowing or lending activities are with reciprocal or in-state partners. Knowing the use both ways helps in evaluating your nonmandated reciprocal arrangements. For example, a reciprocal agreement may no longer be advantageous if you are lending considerably more than you borrow.

You may also want to track the number of different users served, which in lending would be the number of different libraries served and in borrowing might be a breakdown by user status (e.g., faculty, student, staff, graduate, undergraduate). It is often a point of pride for many interlibrary loan units to see how widely they share their collection.

Consider collecting more data than you are required to report to library administration. More details are also useful in managing the operation—for instance, tracking reasons borrowing or lending requests are unfilled. Interlibrary loan management systems allow you to manage this kind of data better, since they make tasks like finding borrowing requests that have been made but have not been received easy to do. Paper files couldn't answer the myriad requests that our new systems make possible. Clever managers use the tools their systems provide to monitor activity.

## Fill Rate

With the basic statistics you record, you can compute a fill rate. You should calculate a fill rate for both borrowing and lending activities. Also, the fill rate for articles might differ from that of loans, so it may be useful to compute them separately to get a complete picture. For example, the total fill rate alone may not show that the fill rate for articles is higher than that for loans. Knowing that discrepancy can allow you to focus on loan fulfillment strategies.

Fill rate is the ratio of requests filled to the number of requests submitted, commonly expressed as a percentage, and represents how successful you are at filling submitted requests. An example of how to calculate a fill rate follows:

**Calculating a Fill Rate**

$$\frac{450 \text{ requests filled}}{525 \text{ requests received}} = .857 \times 100 = 85.7\% \text{ filled}$$

Fill rate can be computed in different ways based on your interpretation of a filled request. Traditionally, the filled requests are those made through the borrowing service and supplied by another library. However, we might want to expand this definition to include requests for material found to be locally available in the library collection, including items found in licensed electronic sources or evenly freely available on the Internet. The requests you don't need to borrow because they are available locally could be viewed as successes, too. This way, you can measure both the success of the staff in borrowing from another library as well as the success in meeting patrons' needs in other ways. These requests reflect the workload of the office, and therefore should not diminish the fill rate by not being counted as part of the total number of filled requests. For instance, if you have a book in your own collection and your patron made an ILL request for it, you might pull the book and put it on hold for the patron. You essentially filled the request from your local collection. You might "cancel" the request and provide the patron with the call number and location of the available book. The book represents both work for the ILL department and a success for the patron, so considering it a filled request might be appropriate. Because patrons may not be able to locate the locally available items they need, and interlibrary loan staff help patrons access this material, a strong argument could be made for considering these requests successes rather than failures.

In the 2002 ARL study of ILL activity,[8] one of the measures used was fill rate (see table 5.4). Although researchers used the traditional definition of "fill rate," they recommended reaching a national consensus. The 1998 ARL study had recommended that requests for locally owned materials not be counted as filled borrowing requests.[9] If you are using the traditional measure, you can compare your unit to these national averages. However, you should still capture all activity.

In managing the activity of the borrowing unit, fill rate might not tell the whole story. For example, when a patron makes a duplicate request or requests something not yet published, should it count against the fill rate? If requests for locally available materials aren't counted as filled requests, perhaps a new, related measure could evolve that counts the collateral work provided for patrons that doesn't result in something borrowed. A new measure might look at the requests received but count as successes all the things the interlibrary loan unit did to meet the patron's need: material borrowed, filled through local circulation, found freely available online, or bought on demand.

Success ratio = number of items provided to patron through the service/number of requests

This method is more oriented toward serving the customer and does not "punish" the unit for the inadequacies of the fill rate statistic. Regardless of how you calculate this statistic, it may assist you in evaluating performance but should not be the only measure used. Compute it to see where you are, then consider how you can be more effective in meeting your goals.

**Table 5.4** ARL 2002 Study: Fill Rates

| | |
|---|---|
| **Total Borrowing** | **86%** |
| Returnables | 85% |
| Nonreturnables | 87% |
| **Total Lending** | **58%** |
| Returnables | 59% |
| Nonreturnables | 57% |

Source: Mary E. Jackson, *Assessing ILL/DD Services: New Cost-Effective Alternatives* (Washington, DC: Association of Research Libraries, 2004), 40.

In lending, some libraries have a similar point of view about the inadequacies of the fill rate. If they can lend something and the borrower declines to pay the fee or is unwilling to meet a restriction, you might still consider the request a success or indicative of the work of the staff. Harry Kriz, interlibrary loan librarian emeritus at Virginia Polytechnic Institute and State University, makes the case that lending fill rate is not a good measure of lending staff performance.[10] He argues that the factors over which his staff had little control (what the borrowers request, what is in use in the collection, and responsibility for data accuracy over which technical services has control such as maintaining serial holdings on OCLC) make lending fill rate an incomplete and inaccurate measure of lending activities. However, it can illuminate issues that, if resolved, might increase the lending unit's productivity.

One example of this strategy is to examine the reasons you say no to incoming lending requests. OCLC WorldCat Resource Sharing libraries can examine the Reasons for No (RFN) report (see figure 3.1). It is available for download from OCLC each month. Additionally, an automated ILL system may be able to report this information. However, in order for this report to be useful, you must provide borrowing libraries with the reason you were unable to fill a request. Providing a reason for not filling a request should be a best practice, both as a courtesy to the borrowing library and for assessment of the lending unit.

To best review cancellation reasons by using the Reasons for No report, export the report to Excel for sorting and counting. You can then review the requests under each reason. Some reasons provide opportunities to improve the number of requests you fill in the future. If you review the requests you didn't fill by each cancellation reason, you might consider changes in policies, target issues for training, or solve problems of access or bibliographic control at your institution. For example, the Not Owned reason might highlight the discrepancy between current inventory as found in the online catalog and the holdings listed for your library on OCLC. Do you have a process in place to ask cataloging to remove your symbol from an OCLC record? If staff are unable to incorporate this practice into the workflow, you might offer to perform this simple task within the ILL unit.

If the most frequent reason article requests are not being filled is Lacking Volume/Issue, this highlights an opportunity to work with the serials department to create local holdings records in OCLC WorldCat. This action may result in savings of staff time and higher fill rate. Reviewing these data on a regular basis might help solve problems in the future. In addition to the Reasons for No report, you can use the OCLC Strategic Union List report to identify the serials requested and the number filled. Another strategy is to customize the ILL management system to record separate cancellation reasons for lending article requests that need Local Holdings Records (LHR) attention and those that don't, in order to regularly pull out the records that need LHR attention. The strategy of working with other departments in your library to improve ILL department performance is discussed later in this chapter.

Although unfilled requests for material that is in use, noncirculating, or on reserve are not failures that can be fixed, searching for lost or not-on-shelf books that might be replaced or withdrawn will improve your lending fill rate and aid your own patrons. Though many systems allow a set number of days for responding to lending requests (e.g., in OCLC it is four), it has become a best practice to say no to a request that you don't find on the shelf after one search, rather than searching a second time for the material. By checking a list of missing items or material not found on the shelf and looking for them later, you might be able to make them available again.

People have argued that if a borrowing library refuses your conditions on an item you could have lent, it should not count as unfilled, because you were willing to lend it under the conditions specified. Check the Reasons for No report to see these requests. Libraries that regularly make requests without meeting your lending fee may not be using OCLC Custom Holdings to identify libraries by fee and should be encouraged to make better use of it or the Policies Directory because those requests are preventable from a lender's perspective.

### Cost Management

A manager should track interlibrary loan fees to be aware of any unexpected costs produced by poor workflow or choice of lenders. Tracking and reporting the amount paid by invoice in both borrowing and lending should be included in cost management processes. If you use the OCLC Interlibrary Fee Management (IFM) system, you can reconcile resource-sharing charges and receipts using the monthly reports made available at OCLC. Even a cursory review of those reports can alert you to charging errors that can be corrected or suggest libraries to pursue for reciprocal relationships.

### Turnaround Time

Getting materials quickly for patrons has always been a goal for interlibrary services. The dramatic decrease in turnaround time (TAT) in the past decade has helped to make ILL a service not only for the scholar working on long-term projects but for all patrons. The 1996 and 2002 ARL studies measured turnaround time and provide some baseline data for comparison with the faster times we are certain to find today (see table 5.5). As Mary Jackson noted, "Turnaround time for mediated borrowing is the one measure that has shown the greatest improvement since 1996. The overall turnaround time is 7.6 calendar days, 49 percent faster than the 1996 mean turnaround time of 15.6 calendar days."[11] Loan turnaround time was found to be on average 9.3 days, reduced from 16.9 days in the earlier study, and turnaround time for copies 6.1 days, much faster that the 14.9 days found in 1996.[12]

Turnaround time should be measured from the time the user makes the request to the time the material is made available to him. Every transaction consists of several steps, and the improvements in overall turnaround time can continue by reducing the time of each step in the process. Let's look at a model of steps in requesting in borrowing and some of the ways time can be reduced.

**Table 5.5** Turnaround Time (TAT) in Two ARL Studies

| Year | Overall TAT | TAT Copies | TAT Loans |
|---|---|---|---|
| 1996 | 15.6 | 14.9 | 16.9 |
| 2002 | 7.6 | 6.1 | 9.3 |

Source: Mary E. Jackson, *Measuring the Performance of Interlibrary Loan Operations in North American Research and College Libraries* (Washington, DC: Association of Research Libraries, 1998).

**Steps in the Borrowing Process**

1. Patron makes request to ILL; unmediated requesting: Direct Request, possible in Rapid
2. Borrowing reviews request and places request to potential lender
3. Lending library receives and reviews request, may say no or continue to process
4. Lending library processes and ships material
5. Borrowing library receives material
6. Borrowing library makes material available to patron

How can turnaround time be improved?

For step 1, web-based request forms have reduced to almost zero the time between the patron initiating the request and the borrowing unit receiving the request.

For step 2, the 2002 ARL study revealed that the range of time required to send a request to the first potential supplier was 1.0 days for fifty-eight of the libraries in the study, but only 7.2 hours at the libraries with the best turnaround time. A solution to this delay is to reduce staff mediation by moving as much mediated ILL traffic as possible to user-initiated services.

Even within traditional OCLC interlibrary loan (i.e., not direct consortial borrowing), using OCLC Direct Request allows requests to be sent to a lender in the WorldCat Resource Sharing system without mediation of borrowing staff. Direct Request uses a profile of rules that determine the criteria by which a request will be automatically sent directly to a potential lending library. It is based on the libraries in your OCLC Custom Holdings groups. You might look at Direct Request as a way of automating a portion of your loan requests and experiment with it. Because a smaller number of requests will be left to mediate, they can be handled more quickly. You can expect a reduction in overall turnaround time, even taking into account that lenders may not be working or shipping on weekends. An improved turnaround time may also result from selecting faster lenders and keeping your preferences for price, speed, and quality in your Custom Holdings groups.

For steps 3 and 4, the burden to reduce turnaround time rests on the lender. Two simple techniques that can reduce turnaround time and improve the service you provide to borrowing libraries are to download requests more frequently and to utilize OCLC deflection rules to deflect requests for material types you do not loan. Printing address labels from a database in an ILL management or shipping system and using couriers reduce the time spent processing material for shipping. See chapter 3 on lending workflow for more discussion of shipping options.

As more requests are made for journal articles that can be filled from online resources, less time is required to pull, scan, and reshelve paper journals. Electronic journals now commonly allow their content to be used to fill ILL requests, though there may be requirements such as printing of the articles and scanning a printed copy (versus sending the electronic copy). Examine your license agreements to determine your rights. Of course, the biggest improvement in turnaround time for articles has been made by the electronic transmission of article requests using Ariel, Odyssey, or e-mail or by posting the article on a web server.

For steps 5 and 6, Odyssey, ClioAdvanced, and Ariel can post articles automatically to a web server, which removes the time and delay necessary for staff to process articles when they come to the borrowing office electronically. These requests are automatically posted to the Web, and the patron is notified moments after the lending library scans and sends the article, regardless whether the ILL office is open.

You may be able to track turnaround time for specific lenders through a management system or through OCLC-provided statistics. OCLC reports the average turnaround time each month on the Borrower Activity Overview Report. This report counts by whole days from the time the request is placed on OCLC until it is updated to "filled" in the system. So although it doesn't measure steps 1 and 6, it is a useful and consistently measured metric of performance that does allow comparison between libraries for steps 2–5.

### User Studies

Another method for evaluating service is to conduct patron surveys. Libraries are turning more to users to find out what is important to them and to ensure that services meet their needs. We can ask our users directly through web survey tools. Patron satisfaction is frequently studied, as is whether a filled request was timely enough to meet the user's needs. Conducting user surveys can be as simple as including a link to an online survey in a notification e-mail or as elaborate as soliciting users and selecting participants based on status, amount of use of the service, or other criteria.

The Higher Education Interlibrary Loan Management Benchmarks report found 15 percent of the libraries sampled had done a user survey in the past four years, but a user study doesn't have to be just about interlibrary service.[13] Some libraries that participate in the ARL LibQUAL+ surveys have added local questions specifically about interlibrary services, using that model to ascertain whether the perceived service meets the desired level of service. Because LibQUAL+ addresses library services, collections, and place, it is an example of how interlibrary services can be just one part of a larger study. User comments about services also come without prompting.

## STAFFING AND HUMAN RESOURCES

There is wide variation in the ways interlibrary loan is done across libraries. It is common for libraries to have a range of employees involved in some aspect of interlibrary loan: students, paraprofessionals, and librarians. As more automation is possible, some processes and functions have really evolved, so the tasks have changed to reduce the amount of clerical processing. Filing and keying data formerly took up much more time, leaving more complex work of a higher level.

The 2002 ARL study concluded that 58 percent of the cost of borrowing and 75 percent of the lending unit costs were staff-related.[14] In a large library it makes sense to have a librarian head the unit because of the level of expertise needed. A librarian can work with other units in the library as a peer, develop relationships with other libraries, reinforce the needs of ILL with library administration, and keep up with developments in the field with an eye out for new ways of doing things that will improve patron service. High-level paraprofessional staff can successfully head the unit too, because they often develop considerable expertise, particularly when they have the support and advocacy of a librarian supervisor.

### Hiring and Training

What's unique about interlibrary services in terms of developing a job description and searching for candidates? We'd like our staff to have a strong service orientation and a belief in the value of the service. An affinity for working with bibliographic information and an attention to detail are also requirements. Candidates without those qualities often are exposed in the application materials. Now, more than ever, a willingness to explore new technology and adapt to changes is also necessary. In my experience, the most important quality to look for is a cooperative spirit—can a candidate get along with people well, be flexible and willing to consider alternatives? This is a helping profession, and many of the bibliographic skills required can be learned if a person can attend to detail. When screening candidates, one useful tactic is to examine their work history for the types of skills required to be successful in the job. Food service, for example, may not seem an obvious indicator of success in interlibrary loan, but it often requires the incumbent to be able to juggle multiple orders or tables, interact with coworkers in other departments (e.g., cooks or busboys), and maintain a good rapport with customers. It is also crucial to discover why a person left such a job. If she left because she did not like the hectic nature of the work or had difficulty remembering customer orders, it may be that she is not a good fit for a job in interlibrary loan.

It is likely that unless they have been reviewed recently, interlibrary loan employees' job descriptions should be evaluated to recognize the higher-level, more technical skills that have overtaken the highly repetitive clerical work of keying and filing. Problem-solving skills are needed for the more difficult bibliographic issues that can arise. The successful interlibrary loan employee will combine these skills with an understanding of the various systems that interact to provide interlibrary services.

### Orientation and Training

Basic orientation of a new hire might start with a review of the library and ILL service website to develop familiarity with published policies. That exploration should lead to an important discussion of the services of the unit. If an ILL manual exists, introduce it as a source to consult, and demonstrate the basic tasks of the position. Show the new person what you do, talking through the steps of handling requests. This discussion also imparts the philosophy of service that you'd like to promote. If you don't have a procedure manual, a new person might draft one to document the steps he learns. Encourage questions and note-taking.

Allowing new staff members to handle requests and demonstrate their thinking will confirm that they are on the right track. Being immediately available when unfamiliar types of issues arise allows requests to be handled swiftly. It can be useful to establish a process for referring requests that need more attention. It may also be helpful to allow a new hire to submit easier requests to build confidence while working together on harder ones. Unfilled requests will help identify areas for further training.

The print bibliographic verification tools that new borrowing staff had to become familiar with as part of their training are not as important today because better tools exist online. Now, a Google search might identify a potential lender for a request, decode a journal abbreviation, and even find the source the patron used to obtain the citation information submitted in the ILL request. Verification in traditional paper tools such as the *National Union Catalog* or the *Union List of Serials in Libraries of the United States and Canada* is needed much less. More frequently, discovering whether or not something is available freely on the Internet, such as in Google Books, is part of the search process.

Students workers can and do perform a great deal of the work in academic interlibrary loan offices. Well-trained students make a significant contribution as they place requests, process incoming material and returns in borrowing, and search, pull, scan, process, and check in returns in lending. They are essential to the team. Their orientation should include an illustration of the overall picture in order to fully understand the contribution of the office. Motivating them with rewards, merit and longevity pay increases, and recognition of special occasions helps retain them.

## Staffing Options

The ARL studies found that the average number of requests handled per full-time equivalent (FTE) employee was 4,394 in borrowing and 10,297 in lending.[15] The Greater Western Library Alliance (GWLA) libraries suggest a staffing guideline of one FTE for each 4,000–5,500 requests received annually for borrowing and one FTE for each 8,000–10,000 requests received annually in lending.[16] Staff time is still the majority of the cost of an ILL transaction, so increasing the number of requests handled per person is a way of reducing the unit cost.

Reviewing each step of the workflow helps streamline actions to reduce the time taken in each part of the process. This reorganization often leads to changes in who does what task and how. In large public or academic libraries, a centralized ILL lending office may receive requests for items that are housed at another location. The traditional approach to this situation uses student workers or pages. These part-time workers report to the central location daily and then travel to various libraries to pick up materials to be loaned or photocopied. We referred to it as sneakernet. However, handling article requests in a decentralized library system can also be done by using staff members and students already working at remote locations in new ways. Rather than spending ten minutes of student wages to send the student to a location, it is more efficient to send the request to the library electronically. In ILLiad, this transmission can be accomplished by e-mail or other routing. This method saves time and also makes the library aware of what is needed from its collection. Local staff may know better than centralized staff how to find material that is not on the shelves and may also be better able to resolve problematic citations given their expertise in the subject.

If the requests are traveling to the distributed locations, it is also possible to install scanners in these locations so that journals do not have to travel back to the central unit for scanning. Distributing the scanning workload is a new way of working with staff in scattered locations and gives those locations new ways to bring their collections to users who are often outside the local institution. Staff and students who don't work directly for interlibrary services may be doing more of the work. This presents a challenge for administrators who should update job descriptions to reflect the changes, develop work priorities, and contribute to staff evaluations. This type of shared responsibility can also happen within the same physical location, but with different departments participating in the process. In some libraries, circulation desk workers may engage in scanning or searching for interlibrary services, or shelving staff may be responsible for pulling requests for interlibrary loan.

In some libraries, people who do interlibrary services may hold joint positions in other units like circulation, reference, or cataloging. Because much of the interlibrary loan workflow is location-independent, it's not surprising to see someone working on ILL requests at another service desk. Many reference desks have slow times, so working on other projects is an efficient use of staff time. Cross-department collaborations enrich our work and maximize the use of personnel, particularly when across-unit staffing allows for a greater number of hours to be covered over the course of a workday.

### WORKING WITH OTHER UNITS IN THE LIBRARY

Over the years, there has been much discussion of where interlibrary services fit into the organizational structure of the library. No single best answer has emerged. In some libraries ILL might be part of reference, circulation, a larger access services unit, or even acquisitions. The service may be split into separate borrowing and lending units as well. It seems that the size of the unit, local practices, staffing, and organizational history might hold clues as to where it is placed in the organization. Keeping borrowing and lending together is desirable to take advantage of the cross-training of staff and their shared understanding of the service. Regardless of where the unit is placed administratively, it is imperative that the manager work with other units in the library to optimize the strength of human resources and to provide the best service possible.

What's in the name, Interlibrary Loan? Because we are describing a service that may be evolving to provide requested documents rather than just borrow from another library, is it time to reconsider the name or even the service's role in the organization? Every interlibrary loan office certainly delivers documents and borrows from other libraries too, but is there a better name than Interlibrary Loan that is immediately well recognized by users and other practitioners? We often see Interlibrary Services or Document Delivery as names to reflect the changes that have taken place. Ask yourself, when you are searching other library websites to find their service, what's clear to you? What name would be clear to your users? Has our role now outgrown our name?

Interlibrary services impact and are impacted by many areas of the library. The services you are able to provide are based on your own collection, your users' access to it, and the records you share. We are fortunate to be in a position to see the big picture of what our patrons need and to help solve problems when our patrons can't access the content we have and come to us for help. We represent all other patrons from other libraries in our lending services. We may also be the most frequent user of our catalog, as we search requests for our patrons and for patrons at other libraries every day. These are some of the reasons that developing strong working relationships with other departments is so important for interlibrary services.

Let's look at some other units in a library and consider how interlibrary services might work with them to provide the best service.

#### Information Technology (IT)

Given the number of systems and software ILL uses daily, ensuring that you have the support of the information technology department in the library is essential. The time-sensitive nature of interlibrary transactions requires immediate resolution of problems that arise. Because some software is unique to interlibrary services, our IT needs differ from those of the rest of the library. Even system upgrades often require careful scheduling with IT in order to provide continuity of service.

Your IT people will need to be involved in decisions about adopting new systems if they are going to be called upon to support them. As interlibrary services become more system-dependent, with more ways to customize service with APIs (application programming interfaces), widgets, and other tools, more technical skills and knowledge will be necessary to fulfill our mission.

### Cataloging

An interlibrary loan unit relies on the work of cataloging because the representation of the library's collection on WorldCat is so important for lending. The use of WorldCat as a union database of holdings for the United States, and increasingly internationally, is pervasive. We rely on WorldCat to help identify who owns a work and who doesn't. This is true for both borrowing and lending as more people use versions of WorldCat to discover material. Although patrons using WorldCat might want to learn whether an item is owned by a library close by, they may also be likely to identify something held only in another country.

Libraries vary widely in maintaining their holdings on OCLC. Ideally, there would be a one-to-one mapping of holdings on WorldCat with the local catalog, so that WorldCat records having your library symbol are in your catalog and vice versa and so that your symbol isn't attached to records you don't own. Whenever a person identifies a record on WorldCat with your symbol, it should be an accurate display of ownership. Increasingly, patrons are using that database as a union catalog for all libraries. This is particularly true for WorldCat Local libraries. Different versions of the database do have different functions. In FirstSearch WorldCat, users can launch a search of the local catalog to find local locations and confirm availability.

For lending, having a process for handling missing or lost material so that a symbol is removed from WorldCat helps reduce requests for which the Reason for No is "not owned" or "missing." "Not owned" is a preventable reason for no, unlike "in use" or "not on shelf." It is important to work with circulation and cataloging to achieve efficient symbol removal for discarded items.[17]

There is much to learn about MARC tags and fields that can help us understand records. Having a colleague in cataloging whom you can ask for help when you don't understand some detail on a bibliographic record is a wonderful support. Such cooperation builds your knowledge and helps to solve the immediate question.

Although cataloging creates records for your local catalog, placing your library symbol on a record allows users elsewhere to find material in the collection. Because cataloging processes vary, work with cataloging staff to learn how they set the library's symbol on records for new materials. Some libraries add their symbol to OCLC when material is ordered, so interlibrary lending might begin receiving requests immediately. We often see many symbols on OCLC records long before the work is even published, and our patrons tell us that dozens of libraries already have the item. However, in searching those local catalogs we see the items are all order records. For libraries that use WorldCat Cataloging Partners, the setting of holdings for a library symbol can be delayed 1 to 180 days to allow enough time for the material to be received, processed, and made available, which would reduce lending requests for items not yet in the collection. This is an ideal solution to reduce requests for material on order, in process, or otherwise considered not owned.

One new function that OCLC has implemented is the ability of lending libraries to deflect requests in two different ways. In the Policies Directory, a lender can easily set up a deflection so that it receives no requests for materials in a particular format, typically e-journals, e-books, media, or loans for serials. But it is also possible to deflect based on maxcost, age of material, or consortial membership. There is even a deflection for all but the "last in the lender string" so that you might only get requests that are unique at your institution or that have been through others first. It takes only a moment to set up deflections in the OCLC Policies Directory, and it is a very powerful tool to reduce requests you would not be able to fill. The requests that are deflected are reported each month as part of the Reasons for No report where the reason will be Auto Deflection, and each type is listed separately. If you've set up deflections, check your Reasons for No report to make sure it's doing what you intended.

The other type of deflection can be added by coding an individual OCLC record with a Local Holdings Record (LHR) to indicate whether a work is requestable as a loan or as a photocopy. LHRs for individual items take some training to create, but deflection can be achieved by adding a code to subtag 20 or 21 of a MARC 008 field to indicate whether loan or photocopy requests will be deflected. Given the work necessary to create an LHR on an individual record, it might be best as a technique for things that will never, rather than temporarily, be lent (e.g., special collections or genealogy materials). LHRs can be batchloaded, too, so you might investigate at the OCLC website and talk with your cataloging department about the potential of LHR deflection.

### Collection Development

Providing information to collection development specialists about what is borrowed or lent can reinforce the role of interlibrary services in the organization. Providing information to subject librarians on what is borrowed can increase their awareness of patrons' interests and inform future buying decisions or result in ordering works borrowed repeatedly. Lists of titles and other reports can be generated from an interlibrary loan system or OCLC report, and the interlibrary loan office can also set up systems for subject specialists to see or create their own reports.

The OCLC Management Statistics report that is produced each month reflects each OCLC request and contains fields like call numbers, date of publication, and language that can be used in our work with collection managers. For example, in my library, we report to our Asian language bibliographers our borrowing and lending statistics for Chinese-, Japanese-, and Korean-language materials based on data from the OCLC Management Statistics report, which they in turn submit to the Council on East Asian Libraries.

Libraries using ILLiad may allow collection managers to access ILLiad's web reports to see the amount of borrowing by department and patron status. It is also common to provide reports from customized queries for subject specialists based on a number of criteria, including books or journal titles requested multiple times. Of course, reporting materials lost in ILL transactions is another way we can work with collection managers, so that replacement can be considered.

There is a body of literature on using interlibrary loan data for collection development that suggests reviewing the frequently requested serials titles as candidates for purchase rather than continued borrowing. Many factors affect the access versus ownership issue, such as monetary costs, patron convenience, and ILL staff time. In many cases, however, the costs of borrowing and copyright fees together are often far less than the cost of a subscription. After canceling a serial, the number of ILL requests for the title can be used to confirm whether the cancellation was appropriate. As article borrowing becomes faster, particularly for libraries participating in RapidILL where fast turnaround is a requirement of participation, and as more purchase options become available from either publishers or commercial document delivery services, there are more choices to explore in support of user needs.

Subject specialists are also an asset when a second eye is necessary for both bibliographic and sourcing issues, helping us find ways to fill difficult requests. It is valuable to be able to call on the language skills of library staff, and their expertise often adds value to the transaction and enhances our professional development. Certainly, being able to refer a patron to a librarian with subject expertise for more help or who can take the time to track down the really obscure reference or provide needed instruction enhances the relationships between and among librarians and patrons.

Because collection managers often determine circulation policies, working with them on reducing restrictions imposed on lending helps make it easier to borrow more freely. Providing ILL statistics to collection managers will help them understand that in order to borrow material from other libraries, it is only fair to lend, too. Our patrons want to borrow dissertations, media, or newspapers on microfilm, so we want collection managers to allow us to lend those materials, too.

### Reference and Circulation

The individuals working the information, circulation, and reference desks market interlibrary services in their work with patrons at the point-of-need. They are on the front line, assisting users with the catalog, databases, and tools that may result in interlibrary borrowing requests. Frontline staff often help patrons sign up for ILL services and educate them on procedures for placing requests. By helping users explore their options for obtaining material, these staff members are partners with interlibrary services. Ensuring that public services staff have correct information on interlibrary policies, basic procedures, and realistic turnaround times for articles and loans helps them accurately offer the service as one of the solutions to meet patron needs.

Your public services staff members also help the patrons of other libraries. As services such as Ask-A-Librarian become more widely available and used, inquiries about "How do I get . . . ?" can also come from users outside the institution. Service desk staffers should be trained in how to answer these questions from externally affiliated patrons, as they may later result in a lending request.

Circulation departments also assist interlibrary service units by keeping material shelved accurately and by having strong processes in place for handling materials that are missing. Ensuring that the catalog reflects a missing item's status and searching for missing materials benefit all patrons but are especially important to ILL. Many borrowing units by policy will not borrow something owned by the library until it is declared missing in the catalog, so the work of circulation helps our staff, our patrons, and the lending unit as well. Searching regularly for missing material so that it is eventually withdrawn and the symbol removed on OCLC contributes to greater success in lending.

### Serials and Electronic Resources

The units that manage journal subscriptions and electronic resources are emerging as important areas for intra-library cooperation, as e-journals have become pervasive in the past decade. The primary question for ILL staff is whether they can lend an article from an electronic journal or database and, if so, with what restrictions? It is essential to work with staff in charge of the licenses to learn these details. It's not just a matter of ascertaining what library has a serial because a library might have access for its own patrons but not have the right to lend the item to other libraries. This scenario is very different from the print world, in which copyright law allows lending. Complicating matters is that although paper and electronic journals may have different ISSNs, databases may use either of them, so requests generated from databases via OpenURL could include either ISSN.

It is common for ILL borrowing offices to still be using OCLC records for paper serials to place requests, although e-journal records for the same content may exist. There are several reasons for this. Many OCLC libraries simply have "deflected" requests for all e-journal records, so that the request never even gets reviewed by the lending library. Other libraries may choose not to fill e-journal requests if they don't know whether they can lend a title. It may also be unclear from the electronic journal record just what years are available electronically. Although we often see online journals starting in the mid-1990s, many publishers also license backfiles. Even if the lending library has a way to know what it can and can't lend, having that information at the point of need for the interlibrary loan unit to make a quick decision on a specific lending request may prove difficult.

As we move toward unmediated article borrowing, we may want to move to preferring records for e-journals so that lenders who have the rights to lend from electronic content can do so quickly and don't have to scan for each request. If an article is available electronically, wouldn't a borrower prefer to get it from a library that can fill it from an e-journal quickly rather than having to find a volume on the shelves and scan it? Having ready access to license rights information will be important in order to make progress in this area.

Even with paper serials, providing accurate information on specific holdings can reduce work for ILL staff. Using Local Holdings Records (LHRs) on OCLC, libraries are now able to indicate their specific serial holdings in addition to indicating ownership. At one time, these data were used for printed lists of serials holdings (e.g., a union list of serials held in a region or by a group). Now, OCLC libraries easily see the specific holdings of libraries in order to target their requests to libraries that own the years or volumes sought. Having accurate serials holdings records allows potential borrowing libraries to make more informed requests based on what volumes or years you own. A best practice for borrowing is to send requests only to libraries that have the needed volume. Libraries that don't indicate their holdings may get fewer requests, while those libraries that do "union list" or create LHRs may get more requests or may reduce the number of requests for issues they do not own. OCLC provides a service for batchloading holdings information, which is now possible for books as well as serials. Libraries can also create or maintain LHRs online through the Connexion browser. Creating LHRs is only part of the workload. Maintaining them for canceled serials requires an ongoing commitment.

It is possible for the ILL office to take on some of the workload of creating and maintaining LHRs, because it is interlibrary loan lending that reaps much of the benefit by reducing the number of requests that can't be filled. For example,

Ohio State University increased its lending fill rate for articles almost 20 percent through creating LHRs.[18] OCLC also reported from a pilot project in 2000 in which ILL staff created holdings records that there was an immediate 3–33 percent increase in fill rate—the more records created, the higher the fill rate.[19]

### Special Collections

We often hear that the future of libraries will be in their special collections: the unique items collected by the library that provide depth and reflect local interests. Working with special collections can be a way for this unit to have its materials more widely used than visits to the collections allow. The Association of College and Research Libraries (ACRL) developed Guidelines for the Interlibrary Loan of Rare and Unique Materials to encourage loans while safeguarding the materials.[20] The guidelines outline the responsibilities of both borrowers and lenders and call for involving the curator with requests on a case-by-case basis. This challenges us to consider working with special collections materials in an interlibrary loan process.

Digitizing on demand might also be a service in which special collections and interlibrary loan could cooperate. Some libraries, like that of the University of Michigan, are already taking lending requests for materials in the public domain and digitizing them, charging the borrowing library for the digitization work but then making it freely available.[21] A review of lending requests might identify special collections materials that other scholars need and help start the conversation about working together.

### Acquisitions

In many ways, our work parallels that of acquisitions, as we both take requests for material and find sources to obtain it. Purchase-on-demand programs have provided another way for acquisitions and interlibrary loan to work together. See the section "Purchase versus Borrow" in chapter 2 for a complete description of the way that ILL interacts with and makes decisions in relation to acquisitions.

## CONCLUSION

Managing interlibrary services offers a wonderful, broad perspective of the interrelationship between library units. It also offers a unique chance to rethink traditional services with an orientation toward the user, to implement new technologies, and to meet users' needs in new ways. Interlibrary service is a core service that is continually strengthened through change and gives us all the opportunity to learn every day. That's why it is such a fulfilling aspect of librarianship.

## NOTES

1. Interlibrary Loan Committee, Reference and User Services Association (RUSA), Interlibrary Loan Code for the United States, revised 2008, by the Sharing and Transforming Access to Resources Section (STARS), www.ala.org/ala/mgrps/divs/rusa/resources/guidelines/interlibrary.cfm.
2. Lee Andrew Hilyer, *Interlibrary Loan and Document Delivery: Best Practices for Operating and Managing Interlibrary Loan Services in All Libraries.* New York: Haworth Information Press, 2006. Published simultaneously as Lee Andrew Hilyer, "Interlibrary Loan and Document Delivery: Best Practices for Operating and Managing Interlibrary Loan

Services in All Libraries; Borrowing," *Journal of Interlibrary Loan, Document Delivery and Electronic Reserve* 16, no. 1–2 (2006): 8–9.
3. Marilyn M. Roche, *ARL/RLG Interlibrary Loan Cost Study: A Joint Effort by the Association of Research Libraries and the Research Libraries Group* (Washington, DC: Association of Research Libraries, 1993).
4. Mary E. Jackson, *Measuring the Performance of Interlibrary Loan Operations in North American Research and College Libraries* (Washington, DC: Association of Research Libraries, 1998).
5. Mary E. Jackson, *Assessing ILL/DD Services: New Cost-Effective Alternatives* (Washington, DC: Association of Research Libraries, 2004).
6. Elaine Sanchez, ed., *Higher Education Interlibrary Loan Management Benchmarks,* 2009–2010 ed. (New York: Primary Research Group, 2009).
7. Paul Kelsey, *Profiles of Best Practices in Academic Library Interlibrary Loan* (New York: Primary Research Group, 2009).
8. Jackson, *Assessing ILL/DD Services,* 41.
9. Jackson, *Measuring the Performance of Interlibrary Loan Operations,* 22.
10. Increasing Lending Fill Rates, www.ill.vt.edu/ILLiadReports/StatEssays/Increasing_Lending_Fill_Rates.htm.
11. Jackson, *Assessing ILL/DD Services,* 52.
12. Jackson, *Measuring the Performance of Interlibrary Loan Operations.*
13. Sanchez, *Higher Education Interlibrary Loan Management Benchmarks,* 30.
14. Jackson, *Assessing ILL/DD Services,* 31.
15. Ibid., 77.
16. Lars E. Leon et al., "Enhanced Resource Sharing through Group Interlibrary Loan Best Practices: A Conceptual, Structural, and Procedural Approach," *Portal: Libraries and the Academy* 3, no. 3 (2003): 425.
17. Anne K. Beaubien, *ARL White Paper on Interlibrary Loan* (Washington, DC: Association of Research Libraries, 2007), 79.
18. Ibid., 71–72.
19. Cathy Kellum, "A Little 'SOUL' Increases ILL Fill Rates," OCLC Newsletter, no. 248 (2000): 33.
20. Guidelines for the Interlibrary Loan of Rare and Unique Materials, www.ala.org/ala/mgrps/divs/acrl/standards/rareguidelines.cfm.
21. Rethinking Resource Sharing, http://rethinkingresourcesharing.org/preconf08/perrywillett_scandemand.ppt.

## BIBLIOGRAPHY

American Library Association. Guidelines for the Development and Implementation of Policies, Regulations and Procedures Affecting Access to Library Materials, Services and Facilities. 2005. www.ala.org/Template.cfm?Section=otherpolicies&Template=/ContentManagement/ContentDisplay.cfm&ContentID=13141.

Association of Research Libraries. *ARL Statistics 2006–2007*. Washington, DC: Association of Research Libraries, 2008.

Beaubien, Anne K. *ARL White Paper on Interlibrary Loan*. Washington, DC: Association of Research Libraries, 2007.

Boucher, Virginia. *Interlibrary Loan Practices Handbook*. Chicago: American Library Association, 1984.

———. *Interlibrary Loan Practices Handbook*. 2nd ed. Chicago: American Library Association, 1997.

Hilyer, Lee Andrew. *Interlibrary Loan and Document Delivery: Best Practices for Operating and Managing Interlibrary Loan Services in All Libraries*. New York: Haworth Information Press, 2006. Published simultaneously as Lee Andrew Hilyer, "Interlibrary Loan and Document Delivery: Best Practices for Operating and Managing Interlibrary Loan Services in All Libraries; Borrowing," *Journal of Interlibrary Loan, Document Delivery and Electronic Reserve* 16, no. 1–2 (2006).

Interlibrary Loan Committee, Reference and User Services Association (RUSA). Interlibrary Loan Code for the United States. Revised 2008, by the Sharing and Transforming Access to Resources Section (STARS). www.ala.org/ala/mgrps/divs/rusa/resources/guidelines/interlibrary.cfm.

Jackson, Mary E. *Assessing ILL/DD Services: New Cost-Effective Alternatives*. Washington, DC: Association of Research Libraries, 2004.

———. *Measuring the Performance of Interlibrary Loan Operations in North American Research and College Libraries*. Washington, DC: Association of Research Libraries, 1998.

Kellum, Cathy. "A Little 'SOUL' Increases ILL Fill Rates." OCLC Newsletter, no. 248 (2000): 33.

Kelsey, Paul. *Profiles of Best Practices in Academic Library Interlibrary Loan*. New York: Primary Research Group, 2009.

Leon, Lars E., et al. "Enhanced Resource Sharing through Group Interlibrary Loan Best Practices: A Conceptual, Structural, and Procedural Approach." *Portal: Libraries and the Academy* 3, no. 3 (2003): 419–30.

Matthews, Joseph R. *The Evaluation and Measurement of Library Services*. Westport, CT: Libraries Unlimited, 2007.

National Library of Australia. *National Resource Sharing Forum and Field Day*. Canberra: National Library of Australia, 2006. www.nla.gov.au.proxy.lib.ohio-state.edu/rsforum/index.html. Includes: Tom Ruthven, *Best Practices in Interlibrary Lending: Results of NRSWG ILL/DD Benchmarking Study*.

Oberlander, Cyril. Transforming Resource Sharing Services (January 13, 2009). http://workshops.rrlc.org/documentview.asp?docID=771.

Roche, Marilyn M. *ARL/RLG Interlibrary Loan Cost Study: A Joint Effort by the Association of Research Libraries and the Research Libraries Group*. Washington, DC: The Association, 1993. http://www.eric.ed.gov/PDFS/ED364242.pdf.

Sanchez, Elaine, ed. *Higher Education Interlibrary Loan Management Benchmarks*. New York: Primary Research Group, 2009.

Stein, Joan. IFLA Guidelines for Best Practice for Interlibrary Loan and Document Delivery. 2006. http://archive.ifla.org/IV/ifla72/papers/073-Stein-en.pdf.

Ward, Jennifer L., Steve Shadle, and Pam Mojfield. "WorldCat Local Impact Summary at the University of Washington." *Library Technology Reports* 44, no. 6 (2008): 2, 4–41. *Academic Search Complete*, EBSCOhost (accessed August 2, 2009).

CHAPTER SIX

# TECHNOLOGY AND WEB 2.0

*Tina Baich and Erin Silva Fisher*

TECHNOLOGY AND WEB 2.0 applications have infiltrated our lives and our libraries. The Internet and other technological advances have allowed for the mass proliferation of information. Publication no longer rests in the hands of the few—anyone with access to a computer can self-publish. This explosion of resources makes it impossible for libraries to purchase everything their users need, which necessitates an increased focus of library resources on access versus ownership. Interlibrary loan plays a crucial role in managing this change in focus.

The ubiquity of technology is a double-edged sword for the ILL practitioner. ILL users are easily able to identify resources from around the world, many of which are difficult to borrow through interlibrary loan. Anyone can locate a potential resource via the Internet whether through Google, WorldCat, or a library catalog. When a user requests an item, she expects to get it. With the speed of new technology, our users are also accustomed to instant gratification in their information-seeking process.

At the same time, however, technology has made the ILL practitioner's job easier. Our systems are no longer paper-based. Virtually all the resources we need to achieve success can be contained on our computers. Citations and holdings are verified via online resources. Communication and collaboration between librarians are more easily accomplished through e-mail and software systems created specifically for our workflows. Articles are scanned and delivered electronically, eliminating waste and speeding turnaround times. The tools to locate and borrow materials have been placed at our fingertips thanks to technology.

This chapter serves as a guide to technological tools that can increase the effectiveness and efficiency of ILL departments.

## ILL MANAGEMENT SYSTEMS

Thanks to technology, ILL practitioners are able to move away from the stacks of paper that once surrounded them. Several software applications are available from which to choose. This section provides background on each to help in your decision-making process.

### OCLC (Online Computer Library Center) Systems

Although some libraries choose to manage their ILL operations using homegrown systems, many libraries use vendor-based products. One of the major providers of ILL management systems is OCLC. Libraries can choose to subscribe to OCLC WorldCat Resource Sharing (WCRS) or license OCLC ILLiad. The internal management capabilities of ILLiad are far greater than those of WCRS, which is primarily a request platform. Although designed to work in conjunction with OCLC WCRS, ILLiad can be used to manage requests outside the OCLC system and, in theory, could be used completely independently of OCLC. According to OCLC, over ten thousand OCLC member libraries use WCRS, while over one thousand libraries and other institutions use ILLiad.

#### *WorldCat Resource Sharing (WCRS)*

WCRS is a web-based platform accessible through the OCLC FirstSearch interface. Subscribers are able to search for requested items in the WorldCat database, view and select potential lenders, and send requests. From the main Resource Sharing screen, ILL staff can view how many requests are in each OCLC status, such as Request Pending, Shipped, Received, and Returned. Benefits of this product include Direct Request, Custom Holdings, and Constant Data profiles, all of which save large amounts of staff time when implemented as they increase automation of routine tasks.

Direct request allows for the unmediated sending of requests into the OCLC ILL system. You can create a direct request profile to specify the types of requests you want sent automatically, including limiting by format. Direct requests must include either an OCLC or ISxN number in order for OCLC to identify the item. Before choosing a lender string and submitting the request, the system checks the item against your own holdings as well as any other library groups you identify in the profile. In order for WCRS to choose the most appropriate lender string, it is helpful if you also create custom holdings groups.

Custom holdings are groups of potential lending libraries defined by the borrowing library. A borrowing library can use a number of criteria to establish these groups, including geographic proximity of the potential lending library, preferred delivery method, and lending fees that may be incurred in the transaction. In addition to working in conjunction with direct request, library holdings are displayed in these customized groups when processing a request manually. Creating groups of preferred lenders has the potential to save both time and money by reducing turnaround times (geographic proximity groups) and fees paid (reciprocal library groups).

Constant Data profiles are another useful WCRS tool. You can establish multiple profiles as needed that automatically populate request forms with information regarding your library, including address information, preferred delivery methods, and the maximum cost you are willing to pay for borrowing an item. You will have one default Constant Data profile, but you can choose another profile at the point of request processing.

*ILLiad*

ILLiad, or Interlibrary Loan Internet Accessible Database, is a software package that provides increased automation of ILL procedures over what is possible in WCRS. Developed in the interlibrary loan department of Virginia Tech University Libraries, ILLiad was launched in phases from 1997 to 1999. Since 2000, it has been a product of Atlas Systems and licensed by OCLC. ILLiad uses a web-based patron interface that allows users to directly submit and track ILL requests without staff mediation. Requests are stored in the database and are accessible to library staff through a separate interface, or client. Transactions are divided into three modules—Borrowing, Document Delivery, and Lending within the client. The ILLiad Client allows staff to search and order on OCLC as well as track requests that fall outside the OCLC workflow. ILLiad also has an integrated scanning utility called Odyssey, which will be discussed later in this chapter. Standard ILL practices can be automated and managed through the use of several companion pieces, including Odyssey Helper, Web Circulation, and the Staff, Billing, Database, and Customization Managers.

Odyssey Helper, released with ILLiad 7.3 in 2008, imports TIF images from a specified networked folder and sends and auto-updates article requests in ILLiad as well as external services such as OCLC or DOCLINE. This capability allows ILL staff to use scanners and software outside the department to create electronic files and batch send them at a later time. Odyssey Helper works with Document Delivery and Lending requests.

Web Circulation, also released with ILLiad 7.3, is a web-based interface that allows access to ILLiad's circulation functions without requiring access to the client. The abilities to check out, mark in transit, check in, and renew can all be controlled through settings in the Customization Manager. Web Circulation users can also search for and retrieve basic request information to respond to patron queries.

The Staff Manager, previously the User Manager, is used to create staff user accounts and set permissions for each staff member. An ILL supervisor can grant access to each of the other ILLiad managers and to specific modules within the client. Although the use of other companion pieces is largely optional, the Staff Manager must be used to configure staff users before they can use the client.

The Billing Manager allows you to generate and print invoices and track payments. Like the ILLiad Client, it is divided into Borrowing, Document Delivery, and Lending modules. A library can choose to use any combination of these modules depending on its fee policies.

The Database Manager is a powerful tool that should be used with caution as its purpose is to delete information from your ILLiad database. There are four tabs within the Database Manager: Transactions, Patrons, Other, and Billing Manager Test Mode. There are three keys in the Customization Manager to help protect transaction data from being deleted based on status and date of request. Patrons can only be deleted if there are no transactions associated with them. A variety of nontransaction and nonpatron information can be deleted using the Other tab. The Billing Manager Test Mode allows you to delete any data created during the testing phase of Billing Manager setup.

The ILLiad system is highly customizable, and most of this is accomplished using the Customization Manager. There are numerous keys that allow you to configure your own settings, including the definition of file names for the various print and e-mail templates used by ILLiad and date sensitive tasks such as the number of days before sending overdue notices. The Customization Manager is also where Web Circulation options are set. There are also tables for Reasons for Cancellation, E-Mail Routing, and Custom Queues, among others, all of which are customizable.

All of the WCRS features previously discussed are also available in ILLiad. Added benefits to using ILLiad include custom web pages, print templates, e-mails, and request queues. The custom e-mail and queue features allow for custom integration of non-OCLC requests into ILLiad. Virtually all requests can be tracked within the system, often with the aid of customizable routing and request queues. For instance, you can create a custom e-mail for frequent suppliers who do not use OCLC such as the National Library of Medicine or for international requests, which also are regularly outside the OCLC workflow. These requests can be routed to a custom queue such as "Awaiting E-mail Response from Lender" as a reminder to follow up at a later date. More information about ILLiad customization can be found at the Atlas Systems website and the IDS Project Workflow Toolkit, which will be described later in this chapter.

ILLiad is also compatible with DOCLINE and RapidILL, two services that will be discussed later in this chapter.

### Other Systems

#### *Clio*

Clio is another ILL management system that operates similarly to ILLiad, working to automate and track interlibrary loan tasks. Clio Software is a family-owned business that has provided interlibrary loan software in the United States since 1994. Clio is completely compatible with WCRS and the National Library of Medicine's DOCLINE system. The software has two versions, ClioBasic and the Clio System. ClioBasic is a solution primarily for staff to manage requests, while the Clio System allows for patron request submission and interaction with an online interface as well as interaction with Ariel and Odyssey electronic delivery methods, which will be discussed later in the chapter.

#### *Relais*

Another popular provider of ILL management products is Relais International. Relais ILL also works to electronically manage interlibrary loan requests with capabilities similar to ILLiad and Clio. For increased productivity, Relais also offers integrated scanning and electronic delivery components.

## SCANNING TECHNOLOGIES

Interlibrary loan operations vastly improved with the creation of scanning hardware and software. Scanners transform printed documents into electronic files that can be sent to lending libraries via a variety of electronic delivery methods. Scanning capabilities have aided in the automation of interlibrary loan operations, improved the speed of delivery, and provided new conveniences for patrons.

### Types of Scanners

The three most common scanning devices within interlibrary loan are flatbed scanners, feeder scanners, and overhead scanners. The construction of each varies, but all three types work similarly to create a digital rendering of a physical document. To use a flatbed scanner, place items face down on the glass component of the machine. Users manually turn pages and repeat the process to scan multipage documents. A feeder scanner, which can be included as a component of a flatbed scanner, automatically feeds loose pages through the machine. Overhead scanners are sometimes referred to as book scanners. With this method, items are placed face up, reducing the impact on the books or other bound items that are being scanned. Overhead scanning also requires less time and effort than flatbed scanning because it is not necessary to remove the book from the scanner in order to turn pages.

### Specialized Scanning Software

Scanners work to digitally render analog data, but additional components are necessary to create usable files. A scanner driver serves as the communication link between a scanner and scanning software application to facilitate the creation and manipulation of digital files. Various drivers exist to interface between scanner hardware and software, and both the software and the hardware must be compatible with the same driver to operate correctly.

Once a digital file has been imported into the designated software application, it is ready to be manipulated according to your needs. For example, pages can be split, rotated, inserted, or deleted.

A variety of scanning software applications have been developed specifically for interlibrary loan. Ariel and Odyssey are the two most common examples; however, new software options to streamline interlibrary loan even more are constantly in development. Ariel and Odyssey products offer both file editing options and mechanisms for electronic delivery through an Internet connection. Ariel, managed by Infotrieve, is a stand-alone product. Odyssey, developed by Atlas Systems, is a component of OCLC ILLiad and can also be used as a stand-alone product.

#### *Ariel*

The Ariel software allows you to scan and send documents to the Ariel workstations of other libraries, or the files can be directly sent to a patron's e-mail address. Documents can also be received from lending libraries using Ariel. The software converts the files from Tagged Image File Format (TIFF) to Portable Document Format (PDF). The PDF file format is preferable for various reasons. TIFF files are typically very large, whereas PDFs are compressed and thus easier to transfer. Additionally, PDF viewing platforms are especially prevalent. As mentioned, Ariel is a stand-alone product, but various ILL management systems have incorporated Ariel into the workflow of their products.

If you are interested in learning more about Ariel, Infotrieve maintains an in-depth user's manual, which can be downloaded from the Ariel Information Center web page (currently located at www4.infotrieve.com/ariel/ricari.html).

#### *Odyssey*

The Odyssey software operates similarly to Ariel, allowing you to scan and send documents to borrowing libraries that are using the same protocol. Documents can also be received from lending libraries that use Odyssey. For libraries using ILLiad, electronic documents received through Ariel or Odyssey are imported into ILLiad, converted to PDFs, and posted to a web server. The OCLC record is automatically updated at this point, if appropriate. An e-mail notification is then generated alerting patrons that their requested article is available. To access the file, patrons simply log on to their online ILLiad account where the file can be accessed.

The free Odyssey stand-alone product does not provide the full range of capabilities mentioned earlier, but it does allow you to edit scanned images, send files between libraries using Odyssey, and convert file formats. Both Ariel and Odyssey products also include an address book component to manage contact information for other libraries. These contacts are usually in the form of IP or e-mail addresses.

## FILE CONVERSION

When dealing with the delivery of electronic documents, you may find it necessary to convert files from one type to another. Ariel and Odyssey, for instance, both use TIFF files for delivery. You may want to convert PDFs to TIFFs to be delivered, or you may need to convert TIFFs to PDFs in the course of troubleshooting. Converting PDFs to TIFFs saves paper and time by eliminating printing and rescanning of articles. There is also the possibility of locating a requested item on a web page, which would require conversion in order to be deliverable.

The National Library of Medicine offers two free file conversion options, DocMorph and MyMorph. DocMorph is a web-based tool that requires no local installation. It is capable of converting over fifty file types into PDF, TIFF, or text files, but it can only convert one file at a time. If you plan to regularly convert a number of files, MyMorph is the better option. This downloadable program is similar to DocMorph, but it allows conversion of multiple files at the same time.

Printing documents to another file type is also a file conversion option. If your Microsoft Office suite includes the Document Imaging program, you can use the Document Image Writer to instantly convert electronic files when needed. The Document Image Writer is a virtual printer that can be used to convert any printable document to a TIFF file. Adobe offers a free PDF Printer Driver plug-in, which also acts as a virtual printer. After downloading, you can convert any printable document to a PDF file. Another option is to install a browser add-on for converting web pages to PDFs.

## OTHER SYSTEMS AND SERVICES

Myriad systems and services exist to assist in specific interlibrary loan functions and can have a high impact on your workflow.

### Article Requesting

Two services that have significantly streamlined article requesting are RapidILL and DOCLINE.

#### *RapidILL*

RapidILL is a growing service option for ILL departments. Although not a management system in and of itself, it can be integrated into the workflows of ILL management systems like ILLiad, Clio, and Relais. Following a 1997 flood that devastated its serial holdings, Colorado State University Libraries needed a way to fill the research needs of its users. RapidILL was developed to fill that need by providing quick, cost-effective, electronic sharing of journal articles. All participating libraries commit to providing twenty-four-hour turnaround times and free article service to the other participants. When a library joins RapidILL, it joins one or more "pods," or groups of libraries, with which it will share. A library can also choose to include document suppliers such as the Linda Hall Library among its potential lenders. These libraries charge a nominal fee to supply articles. All participants' serial holdings are loaded into the RapidILL database to match requests to either the library's own holdings or that of another library in the pod. This matchup prevents libraries from requesting material held in their own collections. Library patrons submit their requests in the library's existing system and are unaware of the use of the RapidILL service as the request platform.

RapidILL further automates the ILL process by using unmediated article request processing. The RapidILL client can automatically check incoming borrowing requests against the holdings database, input local holdings information into the request, and send requests into the RapidILL system for fulfillment. Incoming lending requests also include local holdings information. Together these unmediated actions greatly reduce staff processing time. ILL departments using ILLiad as their ILL management system can choose whether to use the unmediated features designed by ILLiad or those of RapidILL. For more information about RapidILL, visit the RapidILL website at rapidill.org.

### *DOCLINE*

DOCLINE is the interlibrary loan system of the National Library of Medicine (NLM), which facilitates sharing among libraries in the National Network of Libraries of Medicine (NN/LM). The system is primarily for requesting articles from medical and health sciences journals. Developed in 1985, DOCLINE now counts over 3,200 libraries among its users.

DOCLINE consists of three modules. The Institutions module contains institutional records. Each institution's record includes contact and policy information as well as more detailed borrowing preferences that enable the system's automatic routing capabilities. Up-to-date serials holdings are recorded and stored within the serials holdings module, SERHOLD. The Requests module is the third component of DOCLINE. This module is used to place requests and brings together the institutional and holdings data stored in the other two modules to appropriately route requests.

Most articles requested through DOCLINE are based on bibliographic information found in the PubMed/MEDLINE database or through the NLM Gateway. Requests are automatically routed to potential lenders based on institutional preferences and availability. The requesting library can specify the level of service needed, including rush and urgent patient care. DOCLINE is designed to move these requests through the system more quickly. The DOCLINE system can be used in conjunction with a number of ILL management systems, including ILLiad, Clio, and Relais. It is also compatible with a variety of electronic delivery methods, including Ariel. Libraries interested in participating in DOCLINE must first contact the appropriate Regional Medical Library to determine eligibility.

DOCLINE libraries may choose to participate in NLM's Loansome Doc. This web-based request system allows individuals who have established agreements with a DOCLINE-participating library to place requests directly. The DOCLINE library becomes the individual's Ordering Library in the Loansome Doc system. The Ordering Library may supply the requested article from its own collection or obtain it from another DOCLINE library on behalf of the individual. Although NLM does not charge individuals a fee for the Loansome Doc service, the Ordering Library may charge copy or service fees or both.

### Fee Management Systems

In the past, interlibrary loan billing was a complex network of tasks. Invoices needed to be issued for lending requests, and incoming payments for those requests needed to be recorded and processed. Considerable time was also spent receiving invoices for borrowing requests, matching the invoices with corresponding requests, issuing payments, and reconciling accounts. Completing billing tasks required careful oversight and was often time consuming. The labor costs of such tasks also greatly compounded the overall expense of interlibrary loan services.

The billing process was significantly streamlined with the advent of electronic billing methods. Electronic billing eliminates the manual completion of the tedious tasks just mentioned. Several different fee management systems exist today to manage debits and credits for interlibrary loan fees electronically. The most common system is OCLC's ILL Fee Management System (IFM). The Electronic Fund Transfer System (EFTS), created by the University of Connecticut Health Center, is another popular system.

#### *OCLC IFM*

OCLC states that borrowing libraries can save more than $45 by using IFM to eliminate tedious per transaction billing tasks.[1] Any operation using OCLC WorldCat Resource Sharing can use IFM. To begin, simply select IFM and enter a maximum cost within the work form or set your preferences within the Constant Data feature. IFM is a flexible feature. You can easily charge variable amounts based on your interlibrary loan policies. Each month, OCLC will reconcile your account and issue an invoice. The invoice will reflect the credits earned from lending and the charges incurred from borrowing. A minor IFM administration fee is also assessed. You may see three additional line items on your monthly Network or OCLC bill:

- IFM Library to Library borrowing debit—charges your library incurred for borrowing items
- IFM Library to Library lending credit—credits your library receives for supplying items
- IFM administrative fee—a small fee OCLC charges your library for completed borrowing transactions. (Note: The degree to which your network or OCLC bill is affected depends on the extent to which your library uses this option. If you are a large net-lender, your library could decrease its overall bill using the service.)[2]

If you are interested in using IFM to simplify your interlibrary loan billing process, begin by discussing the option with your accounting department. Depending on your library's budget structure, some workflow adjustments may need to be made.

#### *EFTS*

The National Library of Medicine (NLM) uses EFTS as the billing component for the interlibrary loan system DOCLINE. NLM encourages all DOCLINE libraries to participate in the EFTS billing system. EFTS provides the same benefits as OCLC's IFM component. Credits and debits are recorded and reconciled on a monthly basis, which saves individual ILL operations time and money.

To begin using EFTS, visit the University of Connecticut Health Center website to establish an account. The link to the web page is currently https://efts.uchc

.edu, but is subject to change. An online application form must be submitted and accompanied by a Memorandum of Agreement, which needs to be signed by your institution's fiscal officer and mailed to the designated address. A monetary deposit in the amount of one month's estimated borrowing charges is also needed to open the account. Upon completing these steps, contact your Regional Medical Library to change your DOCLINE profile to reflect your participation in EFTS.

To bill borrowing libraries through EFTS, you can enter transaction information within EFTS, use the Transaction File Builder option within DOCLINE, or import a file created by another interlibrary loan management system, such as ILLiad. Each system varies, so consult product documentation to learn about capabilities and setup.

## OpenURL

The OpenURL specification was developed by Herbert Van de Sompel and Patrick Hochstenbach at Ghent University from 1998 to 2000. Van de Sompel and Hochstenbach, who called their project SFX, were responding to the desire to easily link from one electronic resource to articles referenced within it sparked by the increase in electronic publishing seen in the 1990s.[3] At the conclusion of the project, Ghent University sold the rights to the SFX software to Ex Libris, which now markets its version of the OpenURL service under the same name. Several other vendors have developed their own software based on the original open specification developed by Van de Sompel and Hochstenbach. Examples include OCLC WorldCat Link Manager, Serials Solutions 360Link, EBSCO LinkSource, and the UKOLN (Office of Library and Information Networking) OpenResolver. Since its development and widespread acceptance, OpenURL has been adopted as ANSI/NISO Standard Z39.88-2004, the OpenURL Framework for Context-Sensitive Services.

At the most basic level, an OpenURL is a web address, or link, that includes resource-specific metadata in a standardized format. The metadata-enriched URL communicates information about the resource between different information services. The metadata in an OpenURL uniquely identifies a resource. For example, an OpenURL for a journal article might include the ISSN of the journal and volume, issue, and page numbers.

*Example:*
www.yourlibrary.edu/servicename/openurl?genre=article&issn=1072303X&titl
e=Journal+of+Interlibrary+Loan%2c+Document+Delivery+%26+Electronic+R
eserves&volume=17&issue=4&date=20070901&PAGES=63-76

For the OpenURL link to be useful, it must be paired with an OpenURL link resolver. Libraries generally choose to purchase OpenURL link resolver software, often from the same company used to manage electronic resource subscriptions. When a user clicks on an OpenURL link within a discovery tool such as an article database or Google Scholar, the resolver redirects him or her to a web page with options appropriate to that user rather than directing the user straight to the full-text provider. This prevents users from hitting a dead end with nonsubscribed content. If electronic access to a given resource is available freely or through a library subscription, links to that content are presented first. The user is also notified if electronic access is not available. Users are then given the options to search the library's catalog for print versions and, finally, to link to the library's ILL system if neither electronic nor print access is available.

This bridge between discovery tools and ILL management systems is helpful to both users and staff. The metadata included in the OpenURL will auto-populate the request form, which saves the requestor from having to rekey citation information and ensures ILL staff will receive a complete and accurate citation on which to search. The inclusion of the ISBN or ISSN in the metadata makes matching the item easier. ILL staff are less likely to request an incorrect item, which speeds the request and delivery processes. In order for the OpenURL metadata to transfer correctly to ILL request forms, you must map the OpenURL tags in your ILL management system. This mapping instructs the OpenURL in which fields within the request form to place the resource metadata.

## WEB-BASED FINDING AIDS

Whether you are trying to borrow out-of-print monographs, theses or dissertations, foreign titles, or historical documents, web technology has given resource-sharing professionals a plethora of online resources for citation and holdings verification. The likelihood of finding an item freely available online is also increasing as more and more information resources have a digital life.

Many users start their search with Google. Google can also be helpful to ILL staff searching for potential lenders of materials or looking for complete citations. Sub-services of Google like Google Scholar and Google Books can often yield complete citations and even actual documents. This section will discuss these and other web-based finding aids of which you should be aware.

### International Publications

International publications are among the most difficult and time-consuming items to locate and borrow. ILL users can easily locate such items on the Internet but rarely have any concept of the difficulties involved in obtaining them. Luckily for ILL practitioners, the Internet also provides a variety of tools for citation and holdings verification. According to a survey conducted by the ALA RUSA STARS International ILL Committee, the majority of international requests are for items from Canada, Great Britain, Australia, Japan, Germany, and France, all of which have helpful online resources for ILL practitioners.[4]

Whether you are able to locate holdings information in OCLC or not, the national library websites of these countries can assist you in holdings verification and location of policy information. Many developed nations also support online union catalogs to facilitate searching of collections across libraries. Frequently, ILL policy information can be accessed directly from these union catalogs, creating a one-stop shop for information essential to request processing.

### Open Access Materials

Several electronic book repositories are available to assist ILL practitioners in filling requests for texts in the public domain as well as others licensed using Creative Commons licenses. The most well known of these is Google Books. ILL professionals can use Google Books as a source for providing out-of-print and out-of-copyright monographs that would otherwise be unfillable requests. The interface is simple and readily accessible to anyone. The following paragraphs give descriptions of other useful repositories.

Europeana is the shared digital repository of museums, galleries, archives, and libraries across Europe. In addition to texts, it includes images, sounds, and videos.

Gallica is the digital library of the Bibliothèque nationale de France. It provides free access to the written works, images, and sound recordings included in the repository. Gallica is an excellent resource for pre-1900 texts, which would be difficult, if not impossible, to borrow from a French library.

The HathiTrust is a shared digital repository in which major U.S. academic libraries archive their digitized collections. The content of the repository is searchable, and the full-text of public domain items is freely available on the Internet. Though originally a collaboration between the thirteen member universities of the Committee on Institutional Cooperation (CIC) and the University of California system, membership in the HathiTrust is open to all.

The Internet Archive hosts the Wayback Machine, an archive of the World Wide Web. It is also home to extensive archives of moving images, audio, software, educational resources, and text. In addition to housing public domain documents, the Text Archive contains a collection of open access documents, many of which are licensed using Creative Commons licenses. It can be a useful place to find conference papers or reports.

Project Gutenberg is the self-proclaimed oldest repository of open access, full-text public domain texts. This free collection contains over 27,000 free e-books in a number of languages and links to partner projects that take the total over 100,000. The books are available in a number of file formats, including some that are downloadable to an electronic reading device. Project Gutenberg's e-books are in plain text rather than actual page views of the original material.

### Electronic Theses and Dissertations

Theses and dissertations are historically difficult to borrow from granting institutions, but are becoming easier to locate thanks to the advent of electronic theses and dissertations (ETDs). To start, there are the fee-based options of ProQuest's Dissertations and Theses database and Dissertation Express service. Even if you don't subscribe to the Dissertations and Theses database, you can purchase copies of works indexed by ProQuest. However, open access repositories of ETDs are becoming increasingly common.

The Networked Digital Library of Theses and Dissertations (NDLTD) is an international organization "dedicated to promoting the adoption, creation, use, dissemination and preservation of electronic analogues to the traditional paper-based theses and dissertations" (www.ndltd.org). On its website, you can find information about the initiative and how to set up your own ETD program. The NDLTD also offers the ability to search for ETDs and access to research related to NDLTD and ETDs.

Individual academic institutions have developed their own ETD repositories, and an online library catalog or institutional repository search can yield free full-text ETDs. Some national libraries have created their own ETD projects in service of their countries, including Canada and Great Britain. The Theses Canada Portal records electronic access to theses and dissertations when available. Launched in 2009, the British Library's EThOS service offers digitization of U.K. postdoctoral theses. As of August 2009, 105 universities were participating. EThOS has proved extremely popular; it received over 50,000 requests in just the first five and a half months of service.[5]

### Historical Documents

The Library of Congress (LC) is a major repository of historical documents related to United States history. LC continues to place more and more of these American treasures online in an effort to broaden access. Although the online catalog is an excellent resource in and of itself, LC's online collections provide immediate access to a number of primary resources. The American Memory Historical Collections contain resources in a variety of formats that form "a digital record of American history and creativity" (http://memory.loc.gov/ammem/about/index.html). Collections within American Memory range from Frederick Douglass to folk music to World War II maps to woman suffrage. THOMAS is a searchable database of the Congressional Record, bills, and other legislative documents. These are only two of many freely accessible digital projects of the Library of Congress. The wealth of information available is seemingly endless. To browse the LC resources, visit www.loc.gov.

The National Archives and Records Administration (NARA) is the nation's repository for government documents and the most important historical documents of the United States, including the Declaration of Independence and the Constitution. The Archival Research Catalog (ARC) provides online access to the holdings of NARA. Currently, not all of NARA's holdings are indexed in the ARC, but records are added continuously. There is also a searchable, online Guide to Federal Records in the National Archives of the United States. Although you may choose to have users contact NARA directly for record reproductions, its website can help you identify NARA as the appropriate repository to which you should refer users.

Users may also be interested in historical records at a state or local level. State libraries and historical societies are excellent places to locate this type of information. Many of these organizations have online catalogs and websites with information about their ILL policies. Although not all items held by state libraries and historical societies are circulating, ILL practitioners can still provide valuable assistance by locating holding institutions. You may even be able to obtain copies of some documents by contacting the organization directly.

## COMMUNICATION TOOLS

Your library website serves as an essential communication tool. For most users it is the primary gateway to information and services, including interlibrary loan. Yet users often struggle to navigate complex library websites. Enhance your services by creating usable interlibrary loan web pages and providing online assistance.

### Websites

To provide adequate support to online users, ensure that your interlibrary loan web page is easy to locate and easy to use. Provide a link to the interlibrary loan web page on the library's home page. If the web page is located deeper in the website's structure, users are less likely to discover the service, or they can become frustrated while trying to locate the web page. To create a usable web page, consider some of the following guidelines. Clearly display essential content such as request forms and contact information. Define the various services provided by your department in meaningful terminology by avoiding library jargon. For example, if your institution is a member of a library consortium, define the consortium and explain the parameters and benefits of the service. Do the same if you support an internal document delivery service. Provide a list of frequently asked questions and corresponding answers for users seeking assistance. Assist potential borrowing institutions by including relevant information for them on your web page as well.

## Online Assistance

To assist online users at the point of need, employ virtual services such as instant messaging and online tutorials.

### *Instant Messaging*

Within libraries, instant messaging services or chat reference services allow users to seek real-time assistance online by corresponding with a library professional. To communicate via instant messaging, library staff can install and run an instant messaging client to exchange messages with users running similar software. Or staff can embed a chat window directly into any web page with web-based software or a widget (an application or code that can be integrated into a web page), thus allowing users to communicate with a librarian without specialized software. Some of the most popular options currently include Meebo and Digsby.

If your library already provides a chat reference service, provide a link to the appropriate web page from the interlibrary loan page. Consider providing a chat window directly on the interlibrary loan page so users don't need to navigate away from the interlibrary loan web page to ask related questions.

### *Tutorials*

Another way to serve online users at the point of need is to provide asynchronous instruction through online tutorials. Create online tutorials to inform users of interlibrary loan services or to guide users in performing specific interlibrary loan tasks online.

Video tutorials that contain screencasts are especially helpful for virtual users. Screencasts record the displays and actions on a computer monitor. Specialized software allows the video producer to combine the screencasts with audio or textual narration. Providing visual orientation allows users to navigate the library website more effectively and efficiently.

A variety of technologies to create video tutorials now exist. Camtasia and Jing are two common options that are both supported by the company TechSmith. Jing is free, while Camtasia is not. Adobe Captivate is another popular product available for purchase. Investigate the technical specifications of your library's network before pursuing screencast software and creating video tutorials. Adequate technical support and file storage space need to be available to facilitate online access to video files.

## Wikis

Online technologies also exist to support internal communication. A wiki is a website operated by special software that allows for easy, web-based editing without needing any knowledge of HTML or XML. Online content can be created and edited using a text-editor similar to standard word processing programs. The simplicity of a wiki makes it an ideal tool for dynamic departmental collaboration, communication, and knowledge management. The online space can exist as a repository of interlibrary loan policies, a message board, or a how-to guide for difficult tasks, among other uses.

Wiki software options are numerous. Most options are open source and free, within limits. When selecting software, compare the technicalities of each product, as some wikis are more intuitive than others. Investigate the available support and privacy options, among other issues.

Other wikis to support interlibrary loan operations and proprietary software also exist. The IDS Project Workflow Toolkit wiki and the ShareILL wiki are two popular resources. Both wikis aim to share best practices for interlibrary loan operations. The IDS Project Workflow Toolkit is maintained by the Information Delivery Services (IDS) Project, a group of libraries within New York State who are facilitating new and improved methods of sharing resources. The IDS Project Workflow Toolkit contains documentation specifically for ILLiad users. ShareILL includes resources on all aspects of interlibrary loan, and the wiki can be edited by any registered user. Such wikis are extremely helpful for new interlibrary loan professionals searching for free means of training. Unfortunately, these wikis migrate regularly. To locate additional wikis, ask experienced colleagues or search the Internet.

## CONCLUSION

Technology, web-based or otherwise, is rapidly evolving. As technological innovation continues, ILL users will have access to an ever-growing amount of information. This ability to access information and identify resources on a global scale gives ILL an increasingly important role in library services. ILL users need us to help them navigate the vast ocean of information in which they find themselves floating, and sometimes drowning. ILL staff have the skills to locate both commonplace and rare materials and the power to instruct users in how to find information for themselves. We have a responsibility to assist our users by locating the physical materials they identify in a virtual environment. Innovations in technology allow us to further integrate our routine processes into software and web-based systems and to streamline our workflows to focus staff time on fulfilling this responsibility.

It is crucial that ILL practitioners keep up with new technology trends and resources that can impact ILL services and productivity. The ILL community is your greatest resource for knowledge, and that community is stronger than ever. Technology has enabled us to come together in new ways. ILL practitioners can connect on a daily basis to request support, share ideas, and announce innovations in software and services. It is important to be an active member of the community through participation in electronic discussion lists, community portals, and conferences in order to maintain connections to ILL colleagues. By working together as a community, we can harness technology to provide new and improved services to our users and affect positive change in ILL practices.

## WEB RESOURCES

- Ariel Information Center, www4.infotrieve.com/ariel/ricari.html
- Atlas Systems, www.atlas-sys.com
- British Library, EThOS (Electronic Theses Online Service), http://ethos.bl.uk
- DOCLINE, www.nlm.nih.gov/pubs/factsheets/docline.html
- EFTS, https://efts.uchc.edu
- Europeana, http://europeana.eu
- Gallica, http://gallica.bnf.fr
- Google, www.google.com
- Google Books, http://books.google.com
- HathiTrust, www.hathitrust.org
- IDS Project Workflow Toolkit, http://workflowtoolkit.wordpress.com
- Internet Archive, www.archive.org

- Library of Congress, American Memory Historical Collections, http://memory.loc.gov
- Library of Congress, THOMAS, http://thomas.loc.gov
- National Archives and Records Administration, www.nara.gov
- Networked Digital Library of Theses and Dissertations (NDLTD), www.ndltd.org
- OCLC ILLiad 8.0 Documentation, https://prometheus.atlas-sys.com/display/illiad8/ILLiad+8.0+Documentation
- Project Gutenberg, www.gutenberg.org
- RapidILL, www.rapidill.org
- ShareILL, www.shareill.org
- Theses Canada Portal, www.collectionscanada.gc.ca/thesescanada/index-e.html
- United States National Library of Medicine, DocMorph: Electronic Document Conversion, http://docmorph.nlm.nih.gov/docmorph/

## NOTES

1. Simplify Your Billing with Fee Management, OCLC, www.oclc.org/resourcesharing/features/feemanagement/default.htm.
2. ILL Fee Management Frequently Asked Questions, OCLC, www.oclc.org/support/questions/resourcesharing/ifm/.
3. Ann Apps and Ross MacIntyre, "Why OpenURL?" *D-Lib Magazine* 12, no. 5 (May 2006), www.dlib.org/dlib/may06/apps/05apps.html.
4. Sharing and Transforming Access to Resources Section International Interlibrary Loan Committee, "Lending and Borrowing across Borders: Issues and Challenges with International Resource Sharing," *Reference and User Services Quarterly* 49, no. 1 (2009): 58–59.
5. British Library, EThOS Update, www.bl.uk/reshelp/atyourdesk/docsupply/productsservices/theses/blthesesoct2008/ethosupdates/index.html (accessed August 4, 2009).

## BIBLIOGRAPHY


Apps, Ann, and Ross MacIntyre. "Why OpenURL?" *D-Lib Magazine* 12, no. 5 (May 2006), www.dlib.org/dlib/may06/apps/05apps.html.

Barnett, John. 24 Questions about RapidILL. http://raman.library.pitt.edu/magnoliaPublic/Palci/rapid/contentParagraph/04/file/24%20questions%20about%20RapidILL.pdf.

British Library. EThOS Update. www.bl.uk/reshelp/atyourdesk/docsupply/productsservices/theses/blthesesoct2008/ethosupdates/index.html. Accessed August 4, 2009.

Collins, Maria Elizabeth. "DOCLINE: An Overview of the DOCLINE System, Its Functions, Purposes and Descriptions of Participating Libraries." *Journal of Interlibrary Loan, Document Delivery and Electronic Reserve* 17, no. 3: 15–28.

Hodgson, Cynthia. "Understanding the OpenURL Framework." *Information Standards Quarterly* 17 (July 2005): 1–4.

National Information Standards Organization (NISO). *The OpenURL Framework for Context-Sensitive Services.* Bethesda: NISO Press, 2005.

RapidILL. Public Information. https://rapid2.library.colostate.edu/PublicContent/AboutRapid.aspx.

Sharing and Transforming Access to Resources Section International Interlibrary Loan Committee. "Lending and Borrowing across Borders: Issues and Challenges with International Resource Sharing." *Reference and User Services Quarterly* 49, no. 1 (2009): 55–64.

CHAPTER SEVEN

# THE FUTURE OF INTERLIBRARY LOAN

*Cyril Oberlander*

TODAY THERE ARE over 11 million articles and loans moving through resource-sharing library networks each year. Cooperative cataloging, discovery tools, and the maturity of automation in request management for libraries sharing resources have significantly helped users access information and helped libraries reduce operating costs. In the past, ILL requests would be filled in two to four weeks. Now, article requests can be filled in twenty-four to forty-eight hours, and loans within three to six days. Interlibrary loan (ILL) is so successful that authors praise their ILL departments and staff in their acknowledgments; in fact, it is user output, in terms of their reading, learning, research and development, and scholarship, that is an ideal measurement of ILL's success. Through automation, innovation, and cooperation, ILL achieved dramatic decreases in turnaround time while managing dramatic increases in borrowing and lending requests. Perhaps the best illustration of these increases is found in the 2008 Association of Research Libraries (ARL) report that shows the percentage change since 1986: borrowing up 295 percent, lending up 126 percent.[1]

One of ILL's least understood successes is its effective evolution of service and technology within a cooperative framework. Arguably, the key to this success is that ILL must network well to function. In other words, performance is tied directly to the effectiveness of the lending operation of other libraries. Although libraries often place more importance on their borrowing operation because local user satisfaction is essential and immediate, a peculiar dichotomy or shared balance exists with serving internal and external users. For example, the increased use of unmediated borrowing processing has resulted in increased citation verification by the lending libraries. ILL's role has always been multifaceted, with one foot in the local library and the other foot in other institutions and consortia. Similarly, because

ILL's broad service dimension includes providing some reference and technical service, ILL units have a history of constant organizational change produced by shifts in reporting to different units: access, technical, and reference services.

ILL services are a practical and strategic way libraries cooperate, and that cooperation is reinforced by the shared problem solving required to locate and obtain information for users within various networks. Through such problem solving, ILL practitioners have shaped today's ILL processes by migrating from printed national union catalogs to online bibliographic catalogs and from paper requests to OpenURL requests. Tomorrow's ILL will incorporate new services that strategically resolve user needs with robust information supply options. The commercialization of content that has coincided with the phenomenal growth in free open access content has created an Internet-based supply of information that increases the complexity and variation in ILL workflow. Information supply has exponentially expanded beyond library models, and as a result, our users expect more service options. We are at a tipping point for traditional ILL at the peak of its success. To incorporate these emergent supply chains, the new ILL systems must query many external systems and weave the outputs into a shared decision-making framework that creates innovative ways to connect users with information and transforms library services and workflows.

As the information landscape continues to be reshaped by emerging distribution and publishing systems and maturing digitization programs, the strategy best suited for the future of ILL services should remain focused on the user and his request. However, in order to provide more effective service, continued commitment to workflow optimization within networks of resource-sharing partners is not enough; I predict that our future depends on our experimenting with how ILL functions—in particular, developing new internal partnerships within the library (e.g., acquisitions/collection development, digital library production, etc.) and developing workflows with external linkages such as publishers' pay-per-view websites, vendor web services, and a host of free and sharing services available from the Internet.

## INFORMATION SUPPLY—FEE-BASED PARTNERS

Purchasing options are increasingly less expensive and faster than traditional ILL, especially if there are copyright royalty fees or lending charges. In 2009, for example, the copyright royalty for *Agriculture and Human Values* was $33.00, while the cost to buy an article directly from the publisher was $9.64. Similarly, the royalty fee for *Journal of Health Psychology* was $26.00, while pay-per-view was only $15.00. Pay-per-view expanded as publishers increased their discovery via search engines and adopted direct sales of articles via the Internet. This growth will continue as the Internet publishing marketplace for end-user services matures. This development means that for ILL, article purchase is often less expensive than copyright royalty fees combined with lending charges, while providing high-quality color articles faster than borrowing black-and-white articles. ILL systems should incorporate this new reality into their processes and workflow and streamline the determination of when and how to purchase articles using credit cards, EDI (Electronic Data Interchange), IFM, tokens, and the like.

Just-in-time acquisitions or purchase-on-demand for monographs is already a viable alternative to interlibrary loan.[2] For example, in 2007–2008, SUNY Geneseo's ILL placed three borrowing requests for *The Boyhood Diary of Theodore Roo-*

*sevelt, 1869–1870: Early Travels of the 26th U.S. President,* paying a total of $30.00 in lending charges. Meanwhile, used copies were available from Amazon for $2.36. As purchasing books is seriously competing with the cost of borrowing them from libraries, the opportunity to change ILL practice coincides with libraries shifting from just-in-case acquisition models toward just-in-time and user-initiated models. Today's latest e-book license models are designed with various purchase-on-demand strategies; however, selecting physical collections largely remains vendor and librarian driven. Now it is rare that books are unavailable in the marketplace because so many options exist for buying new or used items (many a result of library weeding) as well as digital and physical reprints. Digital and reprint print-on-demand industries are helping ILL obtain rare materials that are inaccessible through borrowing. Given this marketplace reality, when to buy and when to borrow becomes an opportunity for strategic convergence among ILL, acquisitions, and collection development. For example, SUNY Geneseo twice borrowed *Ethnic Conflict in Sri Lanka: Changing Dynamics* for a total of $40.00 in lending charges. That title was available for purchase for only $9.99 and was held by only twenty-two libraries in WorldCat. Geneseo twice missed the opportunity to buy a work needed by users. Purchasing would have diversified the collection held within the network. ILL is in a unique position to facilitate a conversation with users, using data such as cost, uniqueness, and user needs, and with various library stakeholders such as acquisitions and collection development. From these conversations we can develop strategies that help us achieve long-held but rarely achieved cooperative collection development goals.

There are other information suppliers in this marketplace of interest—they are the hybrid fee-based suppliers emerging as resources that can be incorporated into the ILL workflow. These new players include content rental services such as Netflix (www.netflix.com) and McNaughton Books (www.mcnaughtonbooks.com) and peer-to-peer sharing services such as BookMooch (http://bookmooch.com) and PaperBackSwap (www.paperbackswap.com). Increasingly, libraries will use these services to fill certain niche needs that are not easily served by sharing library collections or purchasing for the collection.

## INFORMATION SUPPLY—FREE SUPPLIERS AS PARTNERS

Freely available full text on the Internet is increasingly filling ILL requests and proving a fast and inexpensive source compared to obtaining articles from traditional borrowing processing.[3] Increasingly, ILL staff are using a search engine to find articles on the open Web before submitting a borrowing request. In 2009, ILL units at two libraries using search engines as their first step in the bibliographic searching process reported 5 percent and 6 percent cancellation rates of their article requests because they found the full-text article on the open Web. By 2012, free full text on the Web may fill 20 percent of ILL requests. At various ILL conferences, I ask audience members if they use a search engine to verify citations. Most attendees report using search engines as their first bibliographic verification tool of choice. As a result of using that tool, many ILL units are canceling requests when they find full text and are sending their user the URL to the information resource. Ironically, canceling a "filled" ILL request by supplying the URL to free full text doesn't traditionally count in ILL's fill statistics, and this fact reinforces ILL as exclusively a library-to-library operation. Increasingly, ILL staff are changing how they count filled requests because the outcome is based on the user's perspective, not the supply method or source. As more libraries embrace this definition of a filled request, the workflow and ILL management systems will follow the evolving practice and better integrate search engines and Internet suppliers into existing workflows.

Because free full-text articles and books are increasingly available and found using search engines, the real challenge for ILL practitioners is to resolve the disparate and confusing sources, some with free and some with pay-per-view options. Following are some of the important sources of free full text:

- arXiv (580,000 e-prints), http://arxiv.org
- Directory of Open Access Journals (5,513 journals; 459,876 articles), www.doaj.org
- Electronic Theses Online Service (250,000+ theses), www.ethos.ac.uk
- E-PRINT Network (5.5 million e-prints), www.osti.gov/eprints/
- Google Books (millions of full-view books), http://books.google.com
- HathiTrust (5.2 million volumes), www.hathitrust.org
- Networked Digital Library of Theses and Dissertations (793,000 works), www.ndltd.org
- Open Content Alliance, volumes available at www.archive.org/details/texts/
- OpenDOAR (1,650 repositories), www.opendoar.org
- Project Gutenberg (30,000 books), www.gutenberg.org
- Web archiving:
  - Internet Archive (150 billion pages), www.archive.org
  - Internet Archive's Text Archive (1.8 million works), www.archive.org/details/texts/
  - Pandora, Australia's web archive, http://pandora.nla.gov.au
  - UK Web Archive (127.9 million files), www.webarchive.org.uk/ukwa/info/about/

Looking more specifically at Google Books, a 2006 study of ILL requests at the University of Virginia found 2.6 percent of pre-1923 ILL loan requests could have been filled by Google Books. The following year that percentage grew to 23 percent.[4] The Google Books settlement and the establishment of subscription models for Google Editions further promise to alter the ILL workflow by introducing new opportunities for purchasing content.

ILL's information supply reality is so rich with options that our challenge ahead is creating flexible and quick integration of new sources into ILL and user workflow while thoughtfully balancing automation with cost (time, budget, complexity/noise, scalability, stability). The rapidly evolving landscape may be broadly defined as having four dynamic dimensions (see figure 7.1):

A free domain that includes the plethora of open access repositories, author websites, digital libraries, mass digitization sites, and publisher and online distributor sites

A buying domain that includes various online and physical marketplaces where users or ILL purchase books from book sellers, articles from publishers or distributors, music and video from various online services, and so on

A renting domain with emerging service models that fill niche demands that are problematic for ILL services; libraries may lease collections of popular

**Figure 7.1** Decision and Sense Making in the User and Library Workflow

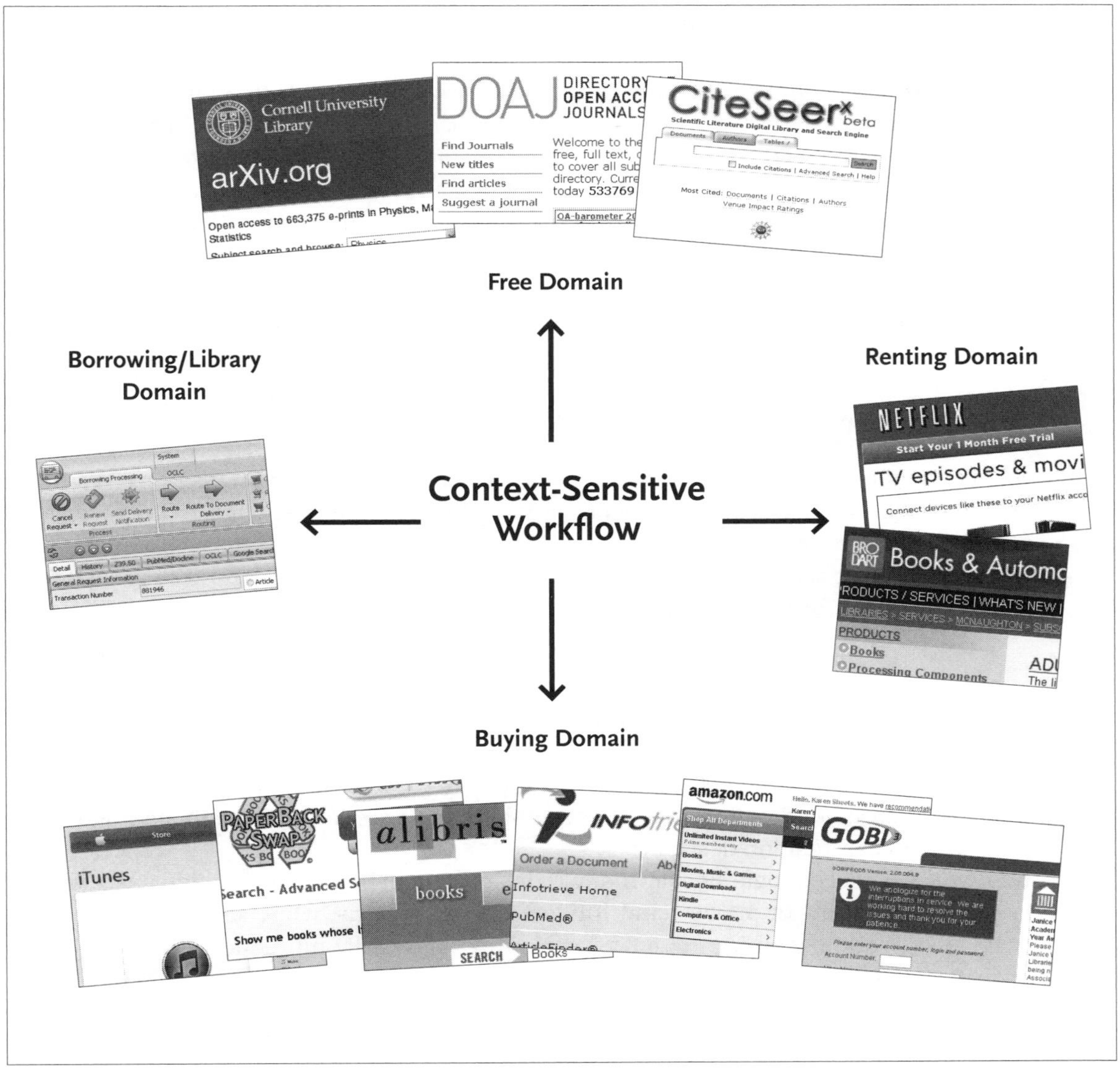

Free Domain

Borrowing/Library Domain

Renting Domain

Context-Sensitive Workflow

Buying Domain

titles and textbooks through a McNaughton plan or supplement their ILL services for videos by renting titles from services such as Netflix

A borrowing domain, best described in the chapter on borrowing; however, paying lending charges resembles the renting domain

## SENSE-MAKING AND INFORMED DECISION WORKFLOW

User adoption of various web services in the free, buying, and renting domains can help us to make sense of or resolve this cornucopia of options. ILL request processing is increasingly developing new context-sensitive workflow that incorporates web searching, often for verification, and purchasing options, often for new books. Most recently, the addition of Addons to ILLiad allows library staff to integrate web services within the ILLiad Client.[5] OpenURL resolvers, OCLC cataloging, book vendors, and search engines are already available.

Together, users and ILL staff will strategically navigate these similar landscapes of information supply to produce innovative strategies that improve mutual informed decision making and expand service. Tools that automate and resolve data help us streamline and bundle options. Book Burro (www.bookburro.org) was an early tool that developed automatic resolution of information supply for end users. This Firefox extension provides quick access to numerous options for book readers, including libraries holding the work by location, price to purchase, peer-to-peer sharing, and other service options. Practically speaking, an end user could easily take a desired book record and choose a delivery option by comparing the display of the nearest library holding that item with the cost of buying it from various vendors or obtaining it for free using peer-sharing networks. Bundling and comparing services will increasingly be configurable by both end users and libraries.

The Getting It System Toolkit, or GIST (http://idsproject.org/Tools/GIST.aspx), is an example of a hybrid ILL workflow, originally developed for ILLiad systems, and is configured to resolve and utilize various information supply options for both end users and library staff. GIST creates opportunities for acquisitions and ILL to share a request management platform that is flexible enough to allow for local practices and powerful enough to simplify and expand traditional acquisitions and ILL. The screenshot in figure 7.2 shows the GIST request form—a customized ILL request form—with information labels added to describe the customizable data feeds from various API sources. GIST web interface widgets include the following:

> The WorldCat API provides users a link to local holdings and estimates delivery time based on the customizable OCLC Holdings groups. Holdings data are used by the staff and ILLiad workflow to provide automated routing based on holdings and collection-building criteria for diversifying holdings in acquisition decisions.
>
> The Google Books, Index Data, and HathiTrust APIs provide users with a variety of preview and full-text linking options, while also providing ILL workflow options to automate routing and easily fill requests with full-text links.
>
> The Amazon API enhances the user's evaluation of the work by adding reviews data and a book cover. It also provides users with a link to a purchasing option and adds the new and lowest-cost prices. With Amazon's API, ILL staff can easily compare the cost of purchasing with the cost of lending charges.

GIST is an example of how ILL tools will incorporate a variety of information supply options from the nonborrowing domains into both the user and staff interfaces. This merging empowers both the user and the staff to meet their goals and allows both to make informed and faster choices about the request.

Amassing useful data and building them into user and ILL workflows is an essential part of the future of ILL. Gathering data such as previews, reviews, and user ratings enhances the user's information discovery and request experience and attempts to answer the problem posed by Danuta Nitecki in 1984: "We are still faced with insufficient techniques for accurately identifying *actual* user needs and delivering the specific information required. Often an identified citation is a hoped-for solution. After waiting for its delivery and examining it, the user may find it to be inadequate and so must begin the search anew."[6]

**Figure 7.2** Getting It System Toolkit: A Hybrid Discovery-Delivery User Interface

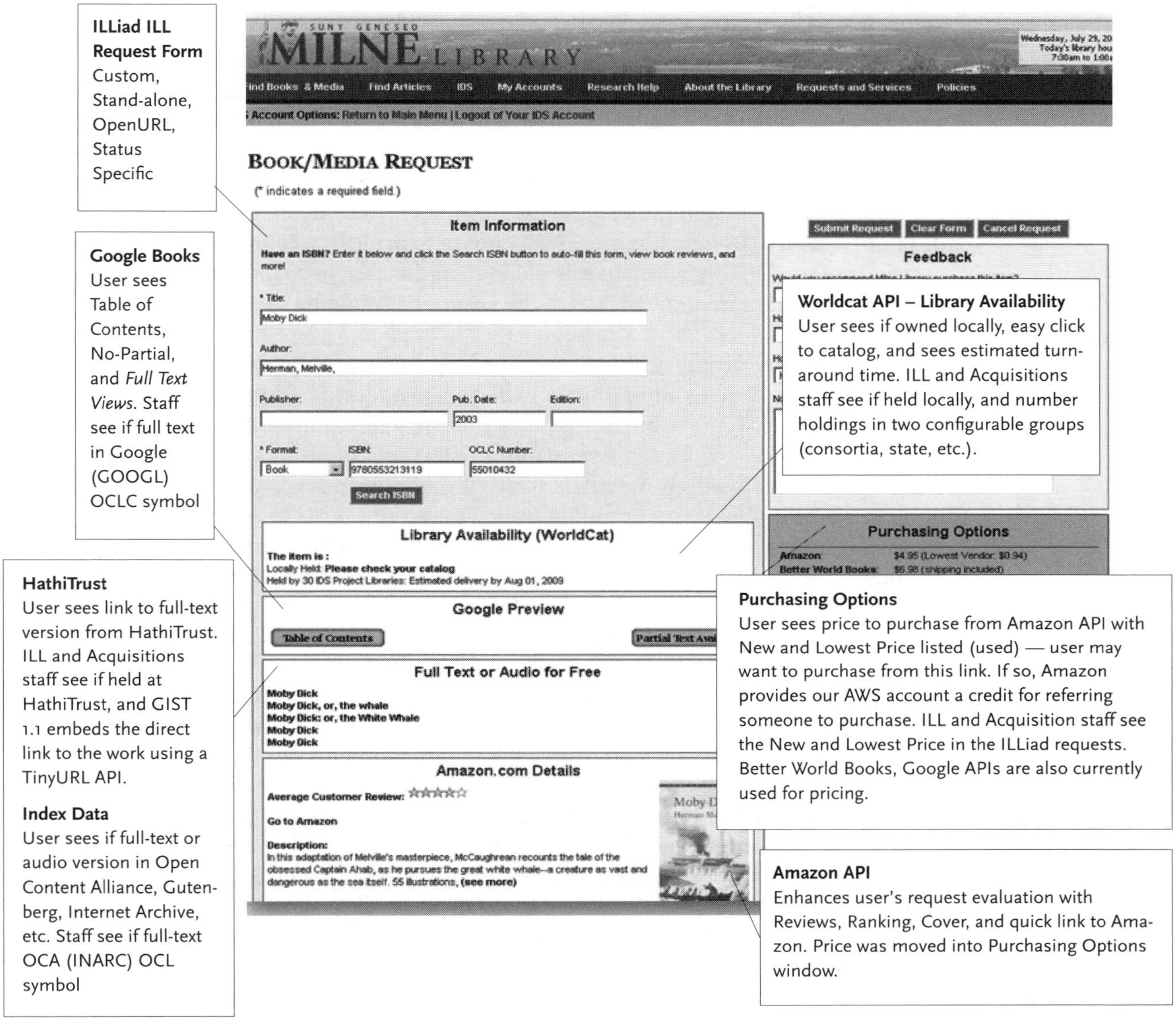

**ILLiad ILL Request Form**
Custom, Stand-alone, OpenURL, Status Specific

**Google Books**
User sees Table of Contents, No-Partial, and *Full Text Views*. Staff see if full text in Google (GOOGL) OCLC symbol

**HathiTrust**
User sees link to full-text version from HathiTrust. ILL and Acquisitions staff see if held at HathiTrust, and GIST 1.1 embeds the direct link to the work using a TinyURL API.

**Index Data**
User sees if full-text or audio version in Open Content Alliance, Gutenberg, Internet Archive, etc. Staff see if full-text OCA (INARC) OCL symbol

**Worldcat API – Library Availability**
User sees if owned locally, easy click to catalog, and sees estimated turn-around time. ILL and Acquisitions staff see if held locally, and number holdings in two configurable groups (consortia, state, etc.).

**Purchasing Options**
User sees price to purchase from Amazon API with New and Lowest Price listed (used) — user may want to purchase from this link. If so, Amazon provides our AWS account a credit for referring someone to purchase. ILL and Acquisition staff see the New and Lowest Price in the ILLiad requests. Better World Books, Google APIs are also currently used for pricing.

**Amazon API**
Enhances user's request evaluation with Reviews, Ranking, Cover, and quick link to Amazon. Price was moved into Purchasing Options window.

## THE FUTURE OF ILL AND ELECTRONIC BOOKS

Two important activities for which resource-sharing systems must develop solutions are lending electronic books and enhancing delivery service options. E-book platforms and format preferences challenge libraries with a cornucopia of confusing options and noninteroperable systems; worse yet, e-books are a significant challenge to resource sharing because few subscription licenses allow for lending. In addition, for those few e-books with ILL rights allowed, the current practice of file sharing chapters is neither a scalable nor long-term solution. Readers will ultimately define the winners or create their own solutions. Future ILL systems and workflow will behave more like digital rights management software and provide a new digital object authentication framework to provide seamless and temporary access to particular titles. In fact, combining this framework with OCLC Direct Request and other unmediated borrowing request systems would result in unmediated lending.

## DELIVERY, DELIVERY, DELIVERY—THE FUTURE OF EXPANDING ILL SERVICES

ILL values getting users what they want at a title or edition level, but we rarely ask users how they want that work delivered (i.e., to home or another location or in a specific format). The richness of information tools and the supply domain is helping to shape user expectations about content and delivery and is encouraging us to rethink delivery problems. Although many users want to visit the library to pick up their books, others would rather we send materials directly to their home, office, or desktop. Sensitive to cost, libraries often choose to limit service models at the cost of user preference; this restriction is obvious in the case of mandating electronic delivery for articles in order to reduce the cost of printing, but less obvious in the case of home delivery.

Home delivery of physical books has a long history and will become a reality again. Though many are familiar with bookmobiles, few know that in 1935, during the Great Depression, Kentucky's Pack Horse Library Project was established as one of the Works Progress Administration's programs in eastern Kentucky.[7] To provide reading materials to rural communities of eastern Kentucky, librarians would ride horses or mules, walk, or even row boats to deliver books and magazines to homes. By 1939, the thirty Packhorse "libraries" served over 48,000 families—almost 181,000 individuals—with 889,694 book circulations (amazing considering that they only had 154,846 books available) and 1,095,410 magazine circulations (again amazing—they only had 229,778 magazines).[8] Past efforts such as these help us realize what our users want and what we are capable of.

Today, the growth of remote user or distance education library services has increased the need for home or office delivery services. The current library-to-library model of interlibrary loan necessitates four shipments per transaction: from lending library to borrowing library, from borrowing library to remote patron and back again, then finally back to the lending library. Options for direct delivery to users will expand in the next few years. If we can reduce the number of shipments involved, libraries can provide faster service to users at lower costs. One of the critical delivery options for the future of ILL is to act as a reformatting service to convert legacy print collections to digital. More libraries are scanning and delivering their print resources because print has replaced microform as the inconvenient format of the twenty-first century. One of the earliest leaders in this hybridization of ILL as document delivery service was Zheng Ye Yang and Texas A&M University Libraries. In June 2002, Texas A&M significantly expanded its services to digitize or reformat its print collections on demand by implementing free electronic document delivery of articles for a campus of 48,000 students. Increasingly, ILL personnel will change ILL services and systems to include more document delivery, digital library production, digitization on demand that supports print-on-demand or reprinting services, and other services such as Optical Character Recognition (OCR). The need for format conversion parallels users' expectations that the content we deliver take the form of their preferred technology and intended use.

## CHANGE FACTORS FOR TOMORROW'S HYBRID SERVICES AND CONTEXT-SENSITIVE WORKFLOW

Today's workflow must evolve new service models because of several key factors in our environment:

- Increased full-text sources will reduce the need for scanning of print.
- Decreased monograph purchasing will necessitate expanding cooperative networks that reduce cost.
- Increased weeding of collections will reinforce the need to expand cooperative collection development and resource-sharing networks and to create last-copy titles with noncirculating or nonlending status.
- Continued maturity of free and fee-based information suppliers will change not only ILL workflow but also the name of ILL service.

As information supply continues to expand options, the variety of information supply channels and demands encourages us to make strategic choices. Making those choices transparent and context sensitive for users and libraries helps all of us make informed decisions. Systems and strategies that bundle data and services in new, flexible, and streamlined ways that help users and library staff achieve their goals will provide a new service framework for libraries. Some current strategies aren't viable in the long term. For example, lending libraries that rely on income from fees will increasingly face challenges because they compete in a market offering better prices and better services (e.g., purchasing eliminates the need for due dates) from book and article distributors. The implication for libraries is that some of the ILL workflow can be reduced or eliminated, while other components can be transformed into new service models. For example, the benefits of merging ILL and acquisitions workflow are now more technically and economically viable because the resources, strategies, and tools are mature enough to make migration to a new service unit possible. Requests become the vehicles to disambiguate library service around the context of user, information, and library service. If a user is placing a book request, the possible activities related to that request may include but are not limited to the following:

- Picking the book up at the desk to read it
- Receiving the book at home to read it
- Accessing the book via laptop as a PDF, a WAV, or an MP3 or via a portable reader of his or her choice
- Sharing the book on course reserves, in group projects or reading groups, with librarians or instructors for discussion, or in social online collaboration tools
- Integrating the book into adaptive learning software, bibliographic management software, or a course management system.

The future of ILL is rich with possible resolution of data and service options that support mutual goals and strategies. For example, the future authors of digital projects and scholarship will require a hybrid of supporting services that foster long-term relationships with authors, researchers, communities, projects, and the like. In that environment, the role of ILL librarian as consultant can grow, and the value of ILL services will be significantly expanded. Group projects that require collections, space, and project support will utilize more sophisticated request management tools. Library consultation services such as these will change the nature of ILL and reference. Reserve and ILL will see more opportunities to develop schedulable on-demand collections that combine library collections and borrowed collections (libraries, faculty personal copies, etc.) with curriculum and instruction. Increasingly, the request management services of libraries will have more in common with customer relations management software because sense making with the user in mind means leveraging strengths of resources and services, and that makes each service request an opportunity to reinforce mutually supportive relationships among users, library staff, resources, and services. That connection bodes well for a vital role for ILL, provided ILL practitioners can leverage their request systems and services to successfully facilitate converging and resolving various library services.

## CONCLUSION

"Though a seamless electronic interlibrary loan function tends to be the present goal, *people* are still what make the difference in interlibrary loan service."[9]

Although ILL personnel bring many strengths to libraries and their users, one that needs special mention is the fundamentally networked approach to problem solving with users and with colleagues from other libraries. We succeed collectively because we depend on each other and focus on delivering what the user requests. Mentoring programs, like those of the IDS Project (http://idsproject.org) and other library cooperatives, will mature in order to accelerate the implementation and sharing of optimized and innovative workflow. Library networks will significantly improve regional professional development to leverage and reinforce local strengths and will expedite developing and sharing expertise in order to make scalable and strategic workflow change effectively and rapidly with the information environment.

ILL practitioners must agree that our operations are no longer just library-to-library transactions. Rather, collectively, we must optimize information delivery services and explore new ways to support users so they can achieve their goals.

We must retain our strengths as successful advanced problem solvers and searchers, willing to innovate, adapt, and redesign our services around user requests. We can do this by asking, "What are users trying to achieve?" and "How can we best serve them?" We must actively shape our service, systems, and workflow, and continue the tradition of effective communication and networking. The expertise we collectively develop is often supported by mentoring and sharing practices and tools. What makes ILL so unique is the scale to which our work is not limited by geography, and the level of shared commitment to best practices exemplifies the role of libraries serving their communities beyond expectations. The future of ILL is being shaped by customer relations and request management strategies.

## NOTES

1. Martha Kyrillidou and Les Bland, comps. and eds., "Graph 3: Supply and Demand in ARL Libraries, 1986–2008," ARL Statistics 2007–2008 (Washington, DC: Association of Research Libraries, 2009), 13, www.arl.org/bm~doc/arlstat08.pdf.
2. Michael Levine-Clark, "An Analysis of Used-Book Availability on the Internet," *Library Collections, Acquisitions, and Technical Services* 28, no. 3 (2004): 283–97; and R. Holley and K. Ankem, "The Effect of the Internet on the Out-of-Print Book Market: Implications for Libraries," *Library Collections, Acquisitions, and Technical Services* 29, no. 2 (2005): 118–39.
3. Heather Morrison, "The Dramatic Growth of Open Access: Implications and Oppor-

tunities for Resource Sharing," *Journal of Interlibrary Loan, Document Delivery and Electronic Reserve* 16, no. 3 (2006): 95–107.

4. Renee Reighart and Cyril Oberlander, "Exploring the Future of Interlibrary Loan: Generalizing the Experience of the University of Virginia," *Interlending and Document Supply* 36, no. 4 (2008): 184–90.
5. ILLiad Integrated Services, https://prometheus.atlas-sys.com/display/ILLiadAddons/.
6. Danuta Nitecki, "Document Delivery and the Rise of the Automated Midwife," *Resource Sharing and Information Networks* 1, no. 3/4 (1984): 95.
7. The "Book Women" of Eastern Kentucky: W.P.A.'s Pack Horse Librarians, www.kykinfolk.com/knott/bookwomen_easternkentucky.htm.
8. Ibid.
9. Virginia Boucher, *Interlibrary Loan Practices Handbook,* 2nd ed. (Chicago: American Library Association, 1997).

## BIBLIOGRAPHY

The "Book Women" of Eastern Kentucky: W.P.A.'s Pack Horse Librarians. www.kykinfolk.com/knott/bookwomen_easternkentucky.htm.

Boucher, Virginia. *Interlibrary Loan Practices Handbook.* 2nd ed. Chicago: American Library Association, 1997.

Holley, R., and K. Ankem. "The Effect of the Internet on the Out-of-Print Book Market: Implications for Libraries." *Library Collections, Acquisitions, and Technical Services* 29, no. 2 (2005): 118–39.

ILLiad Integrated Services. https://prometheus.atlas-sys.com/display/ILLiadAddons/.

Kyrillidou, Martha, and Les Bland, comps. and eds. "Graph 3: Supply and Demand in ARL Libraries, 1986–2008." ARL Statistics 2007–2008. Washington, DC: Association of Research Libraries, 2009, 13. www.arl.org/bm~doc/arlstat08.pdf.

Levine-Clark, Michael. "An Analysis of Used-Book Availability on the Internet." *Library Collections, Acquisitions, and Technical Services* 28, no. 3 (2004): 283–97.

Morrison, Heather. "The Dramatic Growth of Open Access: Implications and Opportunities for Resource Sharing." *Journal of Interlibrary Loan, Document Delivery and Electronic Reserve* 16, no. 3 (2006): 95–107.

Nitecki, Danuta. "Document Delivery and the Rise of the Automated Midwife." *Resource Sharing and Information Networks* 1, no. 3/4 (Spring/Summer 1984): 95.

Reighart, Renee, and Cyril Oberlander. "Exploring the Future of Interlibrary Loan: Generalizing the Experience of the University of Virginia." *Interlending and Document Supply* 36, no. 4 (2008): 184–90.

# CONTRIBUTORS

**TINA BAICH** is an assistant librarian at the University Library of Indiana University–Purdue University Indianapolis where she has been the ILL librarian since September 2006. In addition to supervising the Interlibrary Services department, Tina serves on the Bibliographic and Metadata Services Team as metadata librarian and original cataloger. Tina is especially interested in web-based interlibrary loan finding aids and the impact of open access on interlibrary loan. She has presented on these topics at the OCLC ILLiad International Conference and the Indiana Library Federation Annual Conference and maintains a list of web-based finding aids at http://delicious.com/ILLFindingAids/. She is a graduate of the Indiana University Schools of Library and Information Science and Liberal Arts and holds an MLS and an MA in Public History.

**MARGARET ELLINGSON** is the interlibrary loan team leader at the Woodruff (Main) Library of Emory University and has over twenty-five years of experience in interlibrary loan. In addition to leading the ILL team, she serves as the OCLC ILLiad system manager for all of Emory's libraries. Since 2009 Margaret has been a member of the Steering Committee for the Rethinking Resource Sharing Initiative and chairs its Interoperability Task Force. She was a panel member for the OCLC Research Webinar, *Treasures on Trucks and Other Taboos: Rethinking the Sharing of Special Collections,* and presented "Variations on a Theme: Glimpses of the Current Resource Sharing Landscape" at the NISO Educational Forum, *Collaborative Library Resource Sharing: Standards, Developments and New Models for Cooperating.* She is a past chair of STARS, the Sharing and Transforming Access to Resources Section of the Reference and User Services Association of ALA. Margaret has also served on ALA committees to revise the Guidelines for the Interlibrary Loan of Rare and Unique Materials (2004) and, most recently, the Interlibrary Loan Code for the United States and its Explanatory Supplement (2008). Margaret holds a Master of Librarianship (MLn) degree from Emory University and a BA in English from Queens University of Charlotte, North Carolina.

**ERIN SILVA FISHER** is the document delivery and e-reserves librarian at the University of Nevada, Reno. She received a BA in Communication Studies from Truman State University and an MS in Library and Information Science from the University of Illinois at Urbana-Champaign. She has been working in academic libraries since 2005 and has been involved in interlibrary loan since 2007.

**DENISE FORRO** is head of InterLibrary Services at Michigan State University Libraries. She has worked in interlibrary loan/resource sharing since 1999. She chaired the task force charged to select a statewide delivery for MeLCat, the INN-Reach system for over four hundred libraries in Michigan. Denise instructs practitioners in the use of OCLC WorldCat Resource Sharing (Basic and Advanced) for the Midwest Collaborative for Library Services. She serves as co-coordinator for the ArticleReach Direct group, a consortium of academic research libraries, including a number of international partners. As the 2009–2010 chair of the Sharing and Transforming Access to Resources Section of ALA's Reference and User Services Association, Denise has networked and collaborated with many colleagues during her term of office. She is the author of several articles, including "The Role of an Operations Manager in Interlibrary Loan and Document Delivery Services."

**CINDY KRISTOF** is head of Access Services at Kent State University Libraries in Kent, Ohio. She is responsible for circulation, copyright clearance, interlibrary loan, and reserves, and serves as subject librarian for the College of Technology. She also provides coordination of services to off-campus users. She holds a BA in English from The Ohio State University and an MLS from Kent State University. She has served as an adjunct associate professor for the Kent State University School of Library and Information Science. She is a member of the Copyright Advisory Network Team of ALA's Office of Information Technology Policy. She is a frequent guest speaker on copyright and has led several local copyright workshops for the Kent State University community, OHIONET, and OhioLINK. Since 2008, she has spoken on copyright for the ALA Midwinter RUSA STARS pre-conference ILL workshops.

**JENNIFER KUEHN** is the head of Interlibrary Services at Ohio State University Libraries and has served in that position since 1995. She has also been head of the Social Work Library at Ohio State and has worked in special libraries. Jennifer started working in a public library in 1971 as a student worker and obtained her MLS degree from the Syracuse School of Information Studies.

**SUSAN D. MORRIS** After four years as a schoolteacher, Susan, like so many others in our profession, happily stumbled into a paraprofessional job at the University of Georgia (UGA) Libraries in 1972, starting a chain of events that brought her to her present position. She has thirty-one years of experience in interlibrary loan, first as a paraprofessional and, since 1989, as UGA's interlibrary loan librarian, with short but valuable detours through the acquisitions and reference departments. In her ILL lifetime she has seen the profession evolve from "paper to pixels" and believes that adaptability is the most valuable tool for ILL survival. She has given numerous presentations and chaired several statewide ILL groups, and she was part of the team that developed GIL Express, the University System of Georgia's thirty-five-library direct borrowing system. She has authored several articles on various aspects of ILL in Georgia and has written articles for the innovative digital *New Georgia Encyclopedia*. She holds a BSEd in French from the University of Georgia (1967) and an MLn from Emory University School of Library and Information Science (1984).

**CYRIL OBERLANDER** has been the associate director of Milne Library at the SUNY College at Geneseo since January 2008. Before that, he was the director of Interlibrary Services at the University of Virginia Library (2005–2008), and head of Interlibrary Loan at Portland State University (1996–2005). He has also served as the assistant supervisor and the staff trainer for access services. His consultation experience includes independent consulting services through OCLC and workflow design with various vendors. His research interests include organizational development, workflow design, mobile technology, information visualization, and knowledge systems.

**AMY PAULUS** received a BA in history from Iowa State University in 1996. She then went to the University of Iowa where she earned her MA in Library and Information Science in 1998. Shortly after graduation, Amy began work as a library assistant in the Interlibrary Loan/Document Delivery Department in the Main Library of the University of Iowa and has gradually added to her responsibilities since then. Currently, she is head of Access Services and is responsible for the Interlibrary Loan/Document Delivery, Circulation, Reserve, Media, and Bookstacks departments in the Main Library. Amy is very active professionally and has served on numerous local, state, and regional committees. Her national committee work includes chairing the ALA RUSA STARS Atlas Systems Mentoring Award Committee and the Boucher OCLC Distinguished ILL Librarian Award Committee. She has presented at many local, state, and regional conferences as well as at the ILLiad International Conference and ALA Annual Conference. Publications include a review in the *Journal of Interlibrary Loan, Document Delivery and Electronic Reserve* and an article in *Library Worklife.*

# INDEX